HERBAL PLEASURES

COOKING & CRAFTS

HOW TO USE HERBS IN THE HOME, WITH
OVER 120 ORIGINAL RECIPES, DECORATIONS,
GIFTS AND BATHTIME PREPARATIONS

Herbal *Pleasures*

COOKING & CRAFTS

KATHERINE RICHMOND

HERMES HOUSE

This paperback edition published by Hermes House
an imprint of
Anness Publishing Limited
Hermes House
88-89 Blackfriars Road
London SE1 8HA

A CIP catalogue record for this book is available from the British Library

Publisher: Joanna Lorenz
Project Editor: Penelope Cream
Photographer: Michelle Garrett
Home Economist: Liz Trigg

Previously published as part of a larger compendium,
The Complete Book of Herbs

Typeset by Bookworm Typesetting, Manchester

© Anness Publishing Limited 1995
Updated © 2000
1 3 5 7 9 10 8 6 4 2

CONTENTS

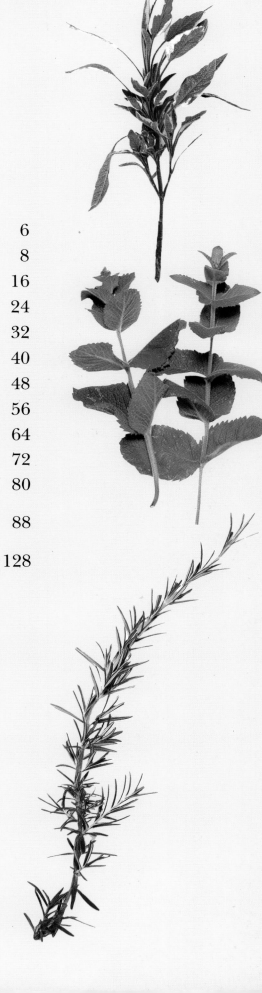

COOKING WITH HERBS

Herb and Chilli Gazpacho

Gazpacho is a lovely soup set off perfectly by the addition of a few herbs.

SERVES 6

1.2 kg/2½ lb ripe tomatoes

225 g/8 oz onions

2 green peppers

1 green chilli

1 large cucumber

2 tbsp red wine vinegar

1 tbsp balsamic vinegar

2 tbsp olive oil

1 clove of garlic, peeled and crushed

300 ml/½ pint/1¼ cups tomato juice

2 tbsp tomato purée

salt and pepper

2 tbsp finely chopped mixed fresh herbs, plus some extra to garnish

1 Keep back about a quarter of all the fresh vegetables, except the green chilli, and place all the remaining ingredients in a food processor and season to taste. Process finely and chill in the refrigerator.

2 Chop all the remaining vegetables, and serve in a separate bowl to sprinkle over the soup. Crush some ice cubes and add to the centre of each bowl and garnish with fresh herbs. Serve with bread rolls.

Pear and Watercress Soup with Stilton Croûtons

Pears and Stilton taste very good when you eat them together after the main course – here, for a change, they are served as a starter.

SERVES 6

1 bunch watercress

4 medium pears, sliced

900 ml/1½ pints/3¾ cups chicken stock, preferably home-made

salt and pepper

120 ml/4 fl oz/½ cup double cream

juice of 1 lime

CROUTONS

25 g/1 oz butter

1 tbsp olive oil

200 g/7 oz/3 cups cubed stale bread

140 g/5 oz/1 cup chopped Stilton cheese

1 Keep back about a third of the watercress leaves. Place all the rest of the watercress leaves and stalks in a pan with the pears, stock and a little seasoning. Simmer for about 15-20 minutes. Reserving some watercress leaves for garnishing, add the rest of the leaves and immediately blend in a food processor until smooth.

2 Put the mixture into a bowl and stir in the cream and the lime juice to mix the flavours thoroughly. Season again to taste. Pour all the soup back into a pan and reheat, stirring gently until warmed through.

3 To make the croûtons, melt the butter and oil and fry the bread cubes until golden brown. Drain on kitchen paper. Put the cheese on top and heat under a hot grill until bubbling. Reheat the soup and pour into bowls. Divide the croûtons and remaining watercress between the bowls.

Warm Chicken Salad with Sesame and Coriander Dressing

This salad needs to be served warm to make the most of the wonderful sesame and coriander flavourings. It makes a simple starter or a delicious light lunch dish.

SERVES 6

4 medium chicken breasts, boned and skinned

225 g/8 oz mange-tout

2 heads decorative lettuce such as lollo rosso or feuille de chêne

3 carrots, peeled and cut into small matchsticks

170 g/6 oz button mushrooms, sliced

6 rashers of bacon, fried and chopped

DRESSING

115 ml/4 fl oz/½ cup lemon juice

2 tbsp wholegrain mustard

250 ml/8 fl oz/1 cup olive oil

65 ml/2½ fl oz/⅓ cup sesame oil

1 tsp coriander seeds, crushed

1 tbsp fresh coriander leaves chopped, to garnish

1 Mix all the dressing ingredients in a bowl. Place the chicken breasts in a shallow dish and pour on half the dressing. Refrigerate overnight, and store the remaining dressing here.

2 Cook the mange-tout for 2 minutes in boiling water, then cool under running cold water to stop them cooking any further. Tear the lettuces into small pieces and mix all the other salad ingredients and the bacon together. Arrange all these in individual serving dishes.

3 Grill the chicken breasts until cooked through, then slice them on the diagonal into quite thin pieces. Divide between the bowls of salad, and add some dressing to each dish. Combine quickly and scatter some fresh coriander over each bowl.

Spinach and Roquefort Pancakes with Walnuts and Chervil

Pancakes make a good starter or buffet dish as you can prepare them in advance. The pancakes can be frozen, but not the filling.

16 PANCAKES

115 g/4 oz/1 cup plain flour

2 eggs

5 tbsp sunflower oil

a little salt

250 ml/8 fl oz/1 cup milk

45 g/1½ oz/3 tbsp butter for frying

FILLING

1 kg/2 lb frozen spinach, thawed

225 g/8 oz/1 cup cream cheese

225 g/8 oz/1 packed cup Roquefort cheese

2 tbsp chopped walnuts

2 tsp chopped chervil

SAUCE

50 g/2 oz/4 tbsp butter

50 g/2 oz/½ cup flour

600 ml/1 pint/2½ cups milk

1 tsp wholegrain mustard

170 g/6 oz/¾ packed cup Roquefort cheese

1 tbsp finely chopped walnuts

1 tbsp fresh chopped chervil, to garnish

1 Process the flour, eggs, oil and salt, slowly adding milk until the mixture has the consistency of single cream. (You may not need to add all the milk.) Let the batter rest in the refrigerator for 1 hour. Put 1 tsp of the butter into a frying pan, and once it has melted swirl it around to coat the surface of the pan.

2 Drop a large tablespoonful of batter into the pan and tilt to spread it around evenly. Cook until golden brown on the bottom, then turn and cook briefly on the other side. Lay the pancake on a wire rack. Cook the others in the same way.

From top: *Spinach and Roquefort Pancakes; Warm Chicken Salad with Sesame and Coriander Dressing*

3 Cook the spinach over a low heat for about 15 minutes. Strain off the water and let the spinach cool. Process in a food processor with the cream cheese and Roquefort until smooth. Turn into a bowl and add half the walnuts and chervil.

4 Preheat the oven to 190°C/375°F/gas 5. Fill all the pancakes and place in a shallow ovenproof dish, rolled tightly and in rows. Make the sauce by melting the butter, adding the flour and cooking for a minute or two. Add the milk and stir constantly until the sauce comes to the boil. Stir in all the other ingredients except the chervil. Pour the sauce over the pancakes and bake for 20 minutes. Serve immediately, sprinkled with chopped chervil and the remaining walnuts.

Spinach, Cognac, Garlic and Chicken Pâté

Pâté is an easy starter, as it can be made well in advance. This smooth version is delicious with warm brown rolls and butter or garlic bread.

12 SERVINGS

12 slices streaky bacon

2 tbsp butter

1 onion, peeled and chopped

1 clove garlic, peeled and crushed

285 g/10 oz frozen spinach, thawed

50 g/2 oz/¾ cup wholemeal bread crumbs

2 tbsp Cognac

500 g/1 lb minced chicken (dark and light meat)

500 g/1 lb minced pork

2 eggs, beaten

2 tbsp chopped mixed fresh herbs, such as parsley, sage and dill

salt and pepper

1 Fry the bacon in a pan until it is only just done, then arrange it round the sides of a 900 ml/1½ pint/1 US quart dish, if possible leaving a couple of slices to garnish.

2 Melt the butter in a pan. Fry the onion and garlic until soft. Squeeze the spinach to remove as much water as possible, then add to the pan, stirring until the spinach is dry.

3 Preheat the oven to 180°C/350°F/gas 4. Combine all the remaining ingredients, apart from any remaining bacon strips, in a bowl and mix well to blend. Spoon the pâté into the loaf tin and cover with any remaining bacon.

4 Cover the tin with a double thickness of foil and set it in a baking pan. Pour 2.5 cm/1 in boiling water into the baking pan. Bake for about 1¼ hours. Remove the pâté and let it cool. Place a heavy weight on top of the pâté and refrigerate overnight.

Beef, Celeriac and Horseradish Pâté

This strongly flavoured pâté would make a good lunch dish as well as a starter.

SERVES 4

500 g/1 lb topside of beef, cubed

350 ml/12 fl oz/1½ cups red wine

85 ml/3 fl oz/⅓ cup Madeira

250 ml/8 fl oz/1 cup beef or chicken stock

2 tbsp finely chopped celeriac

1 tbsp horseradish cream

salt and pepper

2 bay leaves

2 tbsp brandy

170 g/6 oz/¾ cup butter, melted

1 Preheat the oven to 130°C/250°F/gas ½. Place the beef in a casserole. Mix all the other ingredients together except the brandy and butter, and pour them over the beef. Cover tightly and cook for 2 hours.

2 Remove and drain. Strain the liquid and reduce to about 45 ml/3 tbsp. Slice and roughly chop the meat and put it with the reduced liquid in the food processor. Blend until fairly smooth. Add the brandy and a third of the butter. Turn into a pâté dish and leave to cool.

3 Melt the remaining butter, skim any foam off the top and pour over the top of the beef, leaving any residue at the bottom of the pan. Cover the pâté and refrigerate overnight.

Smoked Trout with Minted Grapefruit

Trout and grapefruit make a magical combination, especially with a slight hint of mint.

SERVES 4

1 lollo rosso lettuce

1 tbsp lemon juice

2 tbsp chopped fresh mint, and a few whole leaves for garnish

500 g/1 lb smoked trout skinned, boned and sliced

2 grapefruit, peeled and segmented

120 ml/4 fl oz/½ cup good bottled mayonnaise

1 Toss the lettuce with the lemon juice and half the mint. Arrange on a plate and place the smoked trout among the leaves. Add the grapefruit segments as a decoration.

2 Mix the other half of the chopped mint with the mayonnaise and serve separately in a small bowl, garnished with a mint leaf or two.

Potted Salmon with Lemon and Dill

This sophisticated starter would be ideal for a dinner party. Preparation is done well in advance, so you can concentrate on the main course.

SERVES 6

350 g/12 oz/1¾ cups cooked salmon, skinned

140 g/5 oz/⅔ cup butter, softened

rind and juice of 1 large lemon

2 tsp chopped fresh dill

salt and pepper

75 g/3 oz/¾ cup flaked almonds, roughly chopped

1 Flake the salmon into a bowl and then place in a food processor together with two-thirds of the butter, the lemon rind and juice, half the dill, and the salt and pepper. Blend until quite smooth.

2 Mix in the flaked almonds. Check for seasoning and pack the mixture into small ramekins.

3 Scatter the other half of the dill over the top of each ramekin. Clarify the remaining butter, and pour over each ramekin to make a seal. Refrigerate before serving. Serve with crudités.

Herbed Halibut Mille-Feuille

The crisp puff pastry balances the creamy fish, and the herbs add their own special flavours.

SERVES 2

250 g/9 oz puff pastry
butter for baking sheet
1 egg, beaten
1 small onion
1 tsp fresh ginger, grated
½ tbsp oil
150 ml/¼ pint/⅔ cup fish stock
1 tbsp dry sherry
350 g/12 oz halibut, cooked and flaked
225 g/8 oz crab meat
salt and pepper
1 avocado
juice of 1 lime
1 mango
1 tablespoon chopped mixed
  parsley, thyme and chives, to garnish

1 Roll the pastry out into a square 25 x 25 cm/10 x 10 in, trim the edges and place on a buttered baking sheet. Prick with a fork, then rest it in the refrigerator for at least 30 minutes. Preheat the oven to 230°C/450°F/gas 8. Brush the top with beaten egg, and bake for 10-15 minutes or until golden.

2 Let the pastry cool for a few minutes, then cut it twice across in one direction and once in the other to make six pieces. Leave to cool completely.

3 Fry the onion and ginger in the oil until tender. Add the fish stock and sherry, and simmer for 5 minutes. Add the halibut and crab meat, and season to taste. Peel and chop the avocado and toss in the lime juice. Peel and chop the mango reserving a few slices for garnishing. Add both to the fish.

4 Build up alternate layers of fish and pastry, starting and finishing with a piece of pastry. Serve garnished with herbs and mango slices.

Salmon and Ginger Pie, with Lemon Thyme and Lime

This exceptional pie is highly recommended. This recipe uses salmon's special flavour to the full.

SERVES 4-6

800 g/1¾ lb middle cut of salmon
3 tbsp walnut oil
1 tbsp lime juice
2 tsp chopped fresh lemon thyme
2 tbsp white wine
salt and pepper
400 g/14 oz puff pastry
50 g/2 oz/½ cup flaked almonds
3-4 pieces stem ginger in syrup, chopped

1 Split the salmon in half, remove all the bones and skin, and divide into 4 fillets. Mix the oil, lime juice, thyme, wine and pepper, and pour over the fish. Leave to marinate overnight in the refrigerator.

2 Divide the pastry into two pieces, one slightly larger than the other, and roll out – the smaller piece should be large enough to take two of the salmon fillets and the second piece about 5 cm/2 in larger all round. Drain the fillets. Discard the marinade.

3 Preheat the oven to 190°C/350°F/gas 5. Place two of the fillets on the smaller piece of pastry, and season. Add the almonds and ginger and cover with the other two fillets.

4 Season again, cover with the second piece of pastry and seal well. Brush with beaten egg and decorate with any leftover pastry. Bake for 40 minutes.

From top: *Herbed Halibut Mille-Feuille; Salmon and Ginger Pie*

Cod, Basil and Tomato with a Potato Thatch

With a green salad, it makes an ideal dish for lunch or a family supper.

SERVES 8

1 kg/2 lb smoked cod

1 kg/2 lb white cod

600 ml/1 pint/2½ cups milk

2 sprigs basil

1 sprig lemon thyme

75 g/3 oz/⅓ cup butter

1 onion, peeled and chopped

75 g/3 oz/¾ cup flour

2 tbsp tomato purée

2 tbsp chopped basil

12 medium-sized old potatoes

50 g/2 oz/¼ cup butter

300 ml/½ pint/1¼ cups milk

salt and pepper

1 tbsp chopped parsley

1 Place both kinds of fish in a roasting pan with the milk, 1.2 litres/2 pints/5 cups water and herbs. Simmer for about 3-4 minutes. Leave to cool in the liquid for about 20 minutes. Drain the fish, reserving the liquid for use in the sauce. Flake the fish, taking care to remove any skin and bone.

2 Melt the butter in a pan, add the onion and cook for about 5 minutes until tender but not browned. Add the flour, tomato purée and half the basil. Gradually add the reserved fish stock, adding a little more milk

if necessary to make a fairly thin sauce. Bring this to the boil, season with salt and pepper, and add the remaining basil. Add the fish carefully and stir gently. Pour into an ovenproof dish.

3 Preheat the oven to 180°C/350°F/gas 4. Boil the potatoes until tender. Add the butter and milk, and mash well. Add salt and pepper to taste and cover the fish, forking to create a pattern. If you like, you can freeze the pie at this stage. Bake for 30 minutes. Serve with the chopped parsley.

Tiger Prawns in Filo with Mint, Dill and Lime

Another wonderful combination – the mint, dill and lime blend together to make a magical concoction that will delight everyone who tries it.

SERVES 4

4 large sheets filo pastry

75 g/3 oz/¹⁄₃ cup butter

16 large tiger prawns, cooked and shelled

1 tbsp chopped fresh mint, plus a little more to garnish

1 tbsp chopped fresh dill

juice of 1 lime, plus another lime cut into wedges

1 Keep the sheets of filo pastry covered with a dry, clean cloth to keep them moist. Cut one sheet of filo pastry in half widthways and brush both halves with melted butter. Place one half on top of the other.

2 Preheat the oven to 230°C/450°F/ gas 8. Cut eight of the tiger prawns in half down the back of the prawn and remove any black parts.

3 Place four prawns in the centre of the filo pastry and sprinkle a quarter of the mint, dill and lime juice over the top. Fold over the sides, brush with butter and roll up to make a parcel.

4 Repeat with the other ingredients and place the parcels join side down, on a greased baking sheet. Bake for 10 minutes or until golden. Serve with lime wedges, tiger prawns and mint.

Camembert, Chervil and Plum Profiteroles

Most people are familiar with chocolate profiteroles, but this savoury version is just as delicious and makes an attractive starter.

SERVES 8

300 ml/½ pint/1¼ cups water
140 g/5 oz/⅔ cup butter, cubed
170 g/6 oz/1½ cups plain flour
2 tsp mustard powder
1 tsp powdered cinnamon
4 eggs
75 g/3 oz/¾ cup grated Cheddar
FILLING
225 g/8 oz/1 packed cup Camembert
a little milk
1 tsp fresh chervil, chopped
6 fresh plums, stoned and finely
  chopped
SAUCE
1 x 285 g/10 oz can red plums
½ tsp powdered cinnamon
1 tsp chopped fresh chervil, plus a
  few sprigs to garnish

1 To make the profiteroles, put the water into a saucepan and add the butter. Gently melt the butter, then bring to the boil. As soon as this happens, sieve in the flour, mustard powder and cinnamon. Beat hard with a wooden spoon until the mixture comes away from the sides of the pan.

2 Leave to cool for 10 minutes, then beat in the eggs, one at a time. Add the grated Cheddar, and beat until glossy. Use a large nozzle to pipe blobs about 2.5 cm/1 in across on a greased baking sheet. Bake at 200°C/400°F/ gas 6 for 20 minutes. Cool on a wire rack.

3 Chop the Camembert in small pieces and put in a food processor. Add a little milk and the chervil, and blend to a smooth paste. Remove from the food processor and add the fresh plums.

4 Also make the sauce while the pastries are cooling. Drain the canned plums and stone if necessary. Add them to the cinnamon and chervil in the food processor and blend to a fairly smooth purée.

5 Assemble the profiteroles by halving them and placing some of the Camembert mixture inside. Place the profiteroles on individual plates and dust with a little cinnamon. Serve the sauce separately.

Pork, Thyme and Water Chestnut Filo Parcels

Filo pastry is easy to use and delicious – the light, crisp wrapping makes a simple recipe into a celebration.

MAKES 8

1 tbsp sunflower oil, plus more for
  frying
1 tsp fresh grated ginger
285 g/10 oz pork fillet, finely
  chopped
6 spring onions, chopped
115 g/4 oz/1 cup chopped mushrooms
75 g/3 oz/½ cup chopped bamboo
  shoots
12 water chestnuts, finely chopped
2 tsp cornflour
1 tbsp soy sauce
2 tsp anchovy essence
2 tsp fresh thyme, chopped
salt and pepper
8 large sheets filo pastry
25 g/1 oz/scant 2 tbsp butter, melted

1 Heat the oil and fry the ginger for a few seconds and then add the pork. Stir well and cook until colour changes. Add the spring onions and mushrooms and cook until tender. Add the bamboo shoots and water chestnuts.

2 In a small bowl, mix the cornflour with the soy sauce and anchovy essence. Add to the pan and stir well. Add the chopped thyme, season with salt and pepper, and cook until thickened.

3 Take a sheet of filo pastry and fold in half to make a square. Place two tablespoonfuls of filling across one corner and fold the corner over, then fold in the sides. Brush the folded sides lightly with a little melted butter to help the pastry stick. Complete the roll, and place it join side down on a cloth, then fold the cloth over the top to cover it. Finish all the rolls, putting each one in the cloth as it is made.

4 Heat some oil for semi-deep frying, and fry 2-3 rolls at a time until evenly browned. Drain on absorbent paper and serve hot.

From top: *Camembert, Chervil and Plum Profiteroles; Pork, Thyme and Water Chestnut Filo Parcels*

Lamb Pie, with Pear, Ginger and Mint Sauce

Cooking lamb with fruit is an idea taken from traditional Persian cuisine. The ginger and mint add bite to the mild flavours.

SERVES 6

1 boned mid-loin of lamb, 1 kg/2 lb after boning
salt and pepper
8 large sheets filo pastry
25 g/1 oz/scant 2 tbsp butter
STUFFING
1 tbsp butter
1 small onion, chopped
115 g/4 oz/1 cup wholemeal bread-crumbs
grated rind of 1 lemon
170 g/6 oz/¾ cup drained canned pears from a 400 g/14 oz can (rest of can, and juice, used for sauce)
¼ tsp ground ginger
1 small egg, beaten
skewers, string and large needle to make roll
SAUCE
rest of can of pears, including juice
2 tsp finely chopped fresh mint

1 Prepare the stuffing: melt the butter in a pan and add the onion, cooking until soft. Preheat the oven to 180°C/ 350°F/gas 4. Put the butter and onion into a mixing bowl and add the breadcrumbs, lemon rind, pears and ginger. Season lightly and add enough beaten egg to bind.

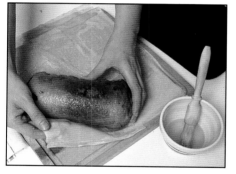

2 Spread the loin out flat, fat side down, and season. Place the stuffing along the middle of the loin and roll carefully, holding with skewers while you sew it together with string. Heat a large baking pan in the oven and brown the loin slowly on all sides. This will take 20-30 minutes. Leave to cool, and store in the refrigerator until needed.

3 Preheat the oven to 200°C/ 400°F/gas 6. Take two sheets of filo pastry and brush with melted butter. Overlap by about 13 cm/5 in to make a square. Place the next two sheets on top and brush with butter. Continue until all the pastry has been used.

4 Place the roll of lamb diagonally across one corner of the pastry, without overlapping the sides. Fold the corner over the lamb, fold in the sides, and brush the pastry well with melted butter. Roll to the far corner of the sheet. Place join side down on a buttered baking sheet and brush all over with the rest of the melted butter. Bake for about 30 minutes or until golden brown.

5 Blend the remaining pears with their juice and the mint, and serve with the lamb.

Steak and Kidney Pie, with Mustard and Bay Gravy

This is a sharpened-up, bay-flavoured version of a traditional favourite. The fragrant mustard, bay and parsley perfectly complement the flavour of the beef.

SERVES 4

450 g/1 lb puff pastry

2½ tbsp flour

salt and pepper

750 g/1½ lb rump steak, cubed

170 g/6 oz pig's or lamb's kidney

25 g/1 oz/scant 2 tbsp butter

1 medium onion, chopped

1 tbsp made English mustard

2 bay leaves

1 tbsp chopped parsley

150 ml/5 fl oz/²⁄₃ cup beef stock

1 egg, beaten

1 Roll out two-thirds of the pastry on a floured surface to about 3 mm/⅛ in thick. Line a 1.5 litre/2½ pint/1½ US quart pie dish. Place a pie funnel in the middle.

2 Put the flour, salt and pepper in a bowl and toss the cubes of steak in the mixture. Remove all fat and skin from the kidneys, and slice thickly. Add to the steak cubes and toss well. Melt the butter in a pan and fry the onion until soft, then add the mustard, bay leaves, parsley and stock and stir well.

3 Preheat the oven to 190°C/375°F/gas 5. Place the steak and kidney in the pie and add the stock mixture. Roll out the remaining pastry to a thickness of 3 mm/⅛ in. Brush the edges of the pastry forming the lower half of the pie with beaten egg and cover with the second piece of pastry. Press the pieces of pastry together to seal the edge, then trim. Use the trimmings to decorate the top in a leaf pattern.

4 Brush the whole pie with beaten egg and make a small hole over the top of the funnel. Bake for about 1 hour until the pastry is golden brown.

Turkey with Apples, Bay and Madeira

This casserole will win you many compliments without the worry of a complicated menu. The unusual apple garnish looks very attractive.

Serves 4

750 g/1½ lb turkey breast fillets, cut into 2 cm/³⁄4 in slices

salt and pepper

50 g/2 oz/4 tbsp butter, plus another 15 g/½ oz/1 tbsp for the apple garnish

4 tart apples, peeled and sliced

60 ml/2 fl oz/4 tbsp Madeira, plus another 30 ml/1 fl oz/2 tbsp for the apple garnish

150 ml/¼ pint/²⁄3 cup chicken stock

3 bay leaves

2 tsp cornflour

150 ml/¼ pint/²⁄3 cup double cream

1 Season the turkey, melt 25 g/1 oz/ 2 tbsp the butter in a pan and fry the meat to seal it. Transfer to a casserole. Preheat the oven to 180°C/ 350°F/gas 4. Add the remaining butter to the pan with two sliced apples, and cook gently for 1-2 minutes.

2 Add the Madeira, stock and bay leaves to the turkey and stir in. Simmer for another couple of minutes. Cover the casserole and bake for about 40 minutes.

3 Blend the cornflour with a little of the cream, then add the rest of the cream. Add this mixture to the casserole and return to the oven for 10 minutes to allow the sauce to thicken.

4 To make the garnish, melt 25 g/ 1 oz/2 tbsp butter in a pan and gently fry the apple slices. Add the Madeira and set it alight. Once the flames have died down continue to fry the apple until it is lightly browned, and garnish the casserole with it.

Beef with Orange Herbal Mustard

The orange herbal mustard is delicious with many different dishes, including cold ham and pork pies. It gives beef a fantastic flavour. This will become a firm favourite.

SERVES 4

45 ml/3 tbsp oil

750 g/1½ lb braising steak cubed

225 g/8 oz/2 cups chopped onion

1 clove garlic, peeled and crushed

2 tbsp flour

300 ml/½ pint/1¼ cups beef stock

2 oranges, plus 1 more for garnish
  and herbal mustard

15 ml/1 tbsp tomato purée

45 ml/3 tbsp Grand Marnier

15 ml/1 tbsp maple syrup

salt and pepper

100 g/4 oz/1 cup sliced mushrooms

HERBAL MUSTARD

2 tbsp mixed fresh herbs, finely
  chopped, such as thyme and chives

juice and grated rind of half an
  orange

3 tbsp Dijon mustard

1 Heat the oil and fry the beef to seal it. Transfer to a casserole. Fry the onion and garlic, drain and add to the casserole. Add the flour to the pan and cook for 1 minute, then add the stock and bring to the boil.

2 Finely slice off the coloured part of the rind of two oranges and chop into small pieces. Squeeze both oranges, and add the juice and the rind to the casserole. Add the tomato purée, Grand Marnier and maple syrup, and season. Preheat the oven to 180°C/350°F/gas 4.

3 Cover the casserole and cook in the oven for at least 1½ hours. Add the mushrooms and return to the oven for another 30 minutes. Serve garnished with slices from half the remaining orange and the herbal mustard described below (remember to grate the orange before cutting it up).

4 To make the herbal mustard, grate the orange rind and mix with the chopped fresh herbs. Then mix in the orange juice and the Dijon mustard. Serve with the beef in a separate dish.

Chicken Stew with Blackberries and Lemon Balm

This delicious stew combines some wonderful flavours, and the combination of red wine and blackberries gives it a dramatic appearance.

SERVES 4

4 chicken breasts, partly boned
salt and pepper
25 g/1 oz/scant 2 tbsp butter
1 tbsp sunflower oil
25 g/1 oz/4 tbsp flour
150 ml/¼ pint/⅔ cup red wine
150 ml/¼ pint/⅔ cup chicken stock
grated rind of half an orange plus
  15 ml (1 tbsp) juice
3 sprigs lemon balm, finely chopped,
  plus 1 sprig to garnish
150 ml/¼ pint/⅔ cup double cream
1 egg yolk
100 g/4 oz/⅔ cup fresh blackberries,
  plus 50 g/2 oz/⅓ cup to garnish

1 Remove any skin from the chicken, and season the meat. Heat the butter and oil in a pan, fry the chicken to seal it, then transfer to a casserole dish. Stir the flour into the pan, then add wine and stock and bring to the boil. Add the orange rind and juice, and also the chopped lemon balm. Pour over the chicken.

2 Preheat the oven to 180°C/350°F/gas 4. Cover the casserole and cook in the oven for about 40 minutes.

3 Blend the cream with the egg yolk, add some of the liquid from the casserole and stir back into the dish with the blackberries (reserving those for the garnish). Cover and cook for another 10-15 minutes. Serve garnished with the rest of the blackberries and lemon balm.

Pork and Mushrooms with Sage and Mango Chutney

The mango chutney and sage leaves add a special flavour to this traditional dish.

SERVES 4

25 g/1 oz/scant 2 tbsp butter
1 tbsp sunflower oil
750 g/1½ lb cubed pork
175 g/6 oz onion, peeled and
  chopped
2 tbsp flour
450 ml/¾ pint/1⅞ cups stock
4 tbsp white wine
salt and pepper
225 g/8 oz mushrooms, sliced
6 fresh sage leaves, finely chopped
2 tbsp mango chutney
1 fresh mango, peeled and sliced, to
  garnish

1 Heat the butter and oil and fry the pork in a pan to seal it. Transfer to a casserole. Fry the onion in the pan, stir in the flour and cook for 1 minute.

2 Preheat the oven to 180°C/350°F/gas 4. Gradually add the stock and white wine to the onion and bring to the boil. Season well and add the mushrooms, sage leaves and mango chutney.

3 Pour the sauce mixture over the pork and cover the casserole. Cook in the oven for about 1 hour, depending on the cut of pork, until tender. Check the seasoning, garnish with mango slices, and serve with rice.

From top: *Pork and Mushrooms with Sage and Mango Chutney; Chicken Stew with Blackberries and Lemon Balm*

Leek and Monkfish with Thyme Sauce

Monkfish is a well known fish now, thanks to its excellent flavour and firm texture.

SERVES 4

1 kg/2 lb monkfish, cubed
salt and pepper
75 g/3 oz/generous ⅓ cup butter
4 leeks, sliced
1 tbsp flour
150 ml/¼ pint/⅔ cup fish or
** vegetable stock**
2 tsp finely chopped fresh thyme,
** plus more to garnish**
juice of 1 lemon
150 ml/¼ pint/⅔ cup single cream
radicchio, to garnish

1 Season the fish to taste. Melt about a third of the butter in a pan, and fry the fish for a short time. Put to one side. Fry the leeks in the pan with another third of the butter until they have softened. Put these to one side with the fish.

2 In a saucepan, melt the rest of the butter, add the remaining butter from the pan, stir in the flour, and add the stock. As the sauce begins to thicken, add the thyme and lemon juice.

3 Return the leeks and monkfish to the pan and cook gently for a few minutes. Add the cream and season to taste. Do not let the mixture boil again, or the cream will separate. Serve immediately garnished with thyme and radicchio leaves.

Fish Stew with Calvados, Parsley and Dill

This rustic stew harbours all sorts of interesting flavours and will please and intrigue. Many varieties of fish can be used, just choose the freshest and best.

SERVES 4

1 kg/2 lb assorted white fish

1 tbsp chopped parsley, plus a few
  leaves to garnish

225 g/8 oz mushrooms

225 g/8 oz can of tomatoes

salt and pepper

2 tsp flour

15 g/½ oz/1 tbsp butter

450 ml/¾ pint/1⅞ cups cider

3 tbsp Calvados

1 large bunch fresh dill sprigs,
  reserving 4 fronds to garnish

1 Chop the fish roughly and place it in a casserole or stewing pot with the parsley, mushrooms, tomatoes and salt and pepper to taste.

2 Preheat the oven to 180°C/350°F/ gas 4. Work the flour into the butter. Heat the cider and stir in the flour and butter mixture a little at a time. Cook, stirring, until it has thickened slightly.

3 Add the cider mixture and the remaining ingredients to the fish and mix gently. Cover and bake for about 30 minutes. Serve garnished with sprigs of dill and parsley leaves.

Lamb and Leeks with Mint and Spring Onions

This is especially good with new season's lamb and organically grown leeks – best of all with leeks from your garden. If you have some home-made chicken stock it boosts the flavour tremendously; if not, use a good quality ready-made stock rather than a stock cube.

SERVES 6

2 tbsp sunflower oil

2 kg/4 lb lamb (fillet or boned leg), cubed

10 spring onions, thickly sliced

3 leeks, thickly sliced

1 tbsp flour

150 ml/¼ pint/⅔ cup white wine

300 ml/½ pint/1¼ cups chicken stock

1 tbsp tomato purée

1 tbsp sugar

salt and pepper

2 tbsp fresh mint leaves, finely chopped, plus a few more to garnish

115 g/4 oz/⅔ cup dried pears, chopped

1 kg/2 lb potatoes, peeled and sliced

30 g/1¼ oz/2 tbsp melted butter

1 Heat the oil and fry the lamb to seal it. Transfer to a casserole. Preheat the oven to 180°C/350°F/gas 4.

2 Fry the onions and leeks for 1 minute, stir in the flour and cook for another minute. Add the wine and stock and bring to the boil. Add the tomato purée, sugar, salt and pepper with the mint and pears and pour into the casserole. Stir the mixture. Arrange the sliced potatoes on top and brush with the melted butter.

3 Cover and bake for 1½ hours. Then increase the temperature to 200°C/400°F/gas 6, cook for a further 30 minutes, uncovered, to brown the potatoes. Garnish with mint leaves.

Stuffed Parsleyed Onions

Although devised as a vegetarian dish, these stuffed onions make a wonderful accompaniment to meat dishes, or an appetizing supper dish with crusty bread and a salad.

SERVES 4

4 large onions

4 tbsp cooked rice

4 tsp finely chopped fresh parsley,
  plus extra to garnish

4 tbsp strong Cheddar cheese,
  finely grated

salt and pepper

2 tbsp olive oil

1 tbsp white wine, to moisten

1 Cut a slice from the top of each onion and scoop out the centre to leave a fairly thick shell. Combine all the remaining ingredients, moistening with enough wine to mix well. Preheat the oven to 180°C/350°F/gas 4.

2 Fill the onions and bake in the oven for 45 minutes. Serve garnished with the extra parsley.

Herbed Chicken with Apricot and Pecan Potato Baskets

The potato baskets make a pretty addition to the chicken and could easily have different fillings when you feel the need for a change.

SERVES 8

8 chicken breast fillets
2 tbsp butter
6 mushrooms, chopped
1 tbsp chopped pecan nuts
115 g/4 oz/½ cup chopped, cooked ham
50 g/2 oz/½ cup wholemeal breadcrumbs
1 tbsp chopped parsley, plus some whole leaves to garnish
salt and pepper
cocktail sticks to secure rolls
SAUCE
2 tsp cornflour
120 ml/4 fl oz/½ cup white wine
50 g/2 oz/¼ cup butter
50 g/2 oz/¼ cup apricot chutney
POTATO BASKETS
4 large baking potatoes
170 g/6 oz pork sausage meat
1 x 225 g/8 oz can apricots in natural juice, drained and quartered
¼ tsp cinnamon
½ tsp grated orange peel
2 tbsp maple syrup
2 tbsp butter
35 g/1¼ oz/¼ cup chopped pecan nuts, plus some pecan halves to garnish

1 Place the chicken breasts between two sheets of greaseproof paper and flatten with a rolling pin or mallet. Melt the butter in a pan and sauté the mushrooms, pecans and ham. Stir in the breadcrumbs and parsley, and season to taste. Divide this mixture between the chicken breasts and roll up and secure each one with a cocktail stick. Refrigerate while making the sauce.

2 Put the potatoes in the oven to bake at 160°C/325°F/gas 3 while you prepare the sauce. Mix the cornflour with a little of the wine to make a smooth paste. Put the remaining wine in a pan and add this paste. Simmer until smooth, and add the butter and apricot chutney and cook for about 5 minutes, stirring constantly.

3 Place the chicken breasts in a shallow ovenproof dish and pour over the sauce. Bake in the oven (do not adjust the temperature) for 20 minutes, basting several times.

4 When the potatoes are cooked through, cut them in half and scoop out the inside, leaving a reasonable layer within the shell. Mash the potato and place in a mixing bowl.

5 Fry the sausage meat and remove some of the fat that comes off. Add the remaining ingredients and cook for 1 minute. Add the sausage meat mixture to the potato and blend gently. Fill the potato shells. Sprinkle the pecan halves over the top, put in the oven with the chicken and bake for another 30 minutes.

6 Remove the chicken breasts from the oven and then drain the sauce into a separate container. Slice the breasts, put on to individual plates and pour the sauce over the top. Serve with the potato baskets and garnish with parsley leaves.

Venison Steaks with Elderberry and Orange

Farmed venison is now widely available. The strong flavour of the meat is well matched by the sweet sauce.

SERVES 4

4 venison steaks, 170-225 g/6-8 oz each
olive oil for basting
black pepper
salt
2 tbsp red wine
4 tbsp orange juice, plus slices of orange to garnish
2 tbsp elderberry jelly
sprigs of parsley, to garnish

1 Pound the venison steaks a little with a meat mallet to make the meat more tender.

2 Brush with olive oil and season with freshly ground black pepper. Grill under a high heat until done to your taste. Sprinkle with a little salt.

3 In a pan, reduce the red wine, then add the orange juice and elderberry jelly and simmer for 10 minutes. Pour over the steaks and garnish with slices of orange and parsley sprigs.

From top: *Venison Steaks with Elderberry and Orange; Herbed Chicken with Apricot and Pecan Potato Baskets*

Chicken with Sloe Gin and Juniper

 Juniper is used in the manufacture of gin, and the reinforcement of the flavour by using both sloe gin and juniper is delicious. Sloe gin is easy to make, but can also be bought ready-made.

SERVES 8

2 tbsp butter
2 tbsp sunflower oil
8 chicken breast fillets
350 g/12 oz carrots, cooked
1 clove garlic, peeled and crushed
1 tbsp finely chopped parsley
60 ml/2 fl oz/¼ cup chicken stock
60 ml/2 fl oz/¼ cup red wine
60 ml/2 fl oz/¼ cup sloe gin
1 tsp crushed juniper berries
salt and pepper
1 bunch basil, to garnish

1 Melt the butter with the oil in a pan, and sauté the chicken until browned on all sides.

2 In a food processor, combine all the remaining ingredients except the watercress, and blend to a smooth purée. If the mixture seems too thick add a little more red wine or water until a thinner consistency is reached.

3 Put the chicken breasts in a pan, pour the sauce over the top and cook until the chicken is cooked through – about 15 minutes. Adjust the seasoning and serve garnished with chopped fresh basil.

Duck Breasts with Red Plums, Cinnamon and Coriander

Duck breasts can be bought separately, which makes this dish very easy to prepare.

SERVES 4

4 duck breasts, 175 g/6 oz each, skinned

salt

2 tsp stick cinnamon, crushed

50 g/2 oz/¼ cup butter

1 tbsp plum brandy (or Cognac)

250 ml/8 fl oz/1 cup chicken stock

250 ml/8 fl oz/1 cup double cream

pepper

6 fresh red plums, stoned and sliced

6 sprigs coriander leaves, plus some extra to garnish

1 Preheat the oven to 190°C/375°F/ gas 5. Score the duck breasts and sprinkle with salt. Press the crushed cinnamon on to both sides of the duck breasts. Melt half the butter in a pan and fry them on both sides to seal, then place in an ovenproof dish with the butter and bake for 6-7 minutes.

2 Remove the dish from the oven and return the contents to the pan. Add the brandy and set it alight. When the flames have died down, remove from the pan and keep warm. Add the stock and cream to the pan and simmer gently until reduced and thick. Adjust the seasoning.

3 Reserve a few plum slices for garnishing. In a pan, melt the other half of the butter and fry the plums and coriander, just enough to cook the fruit through. Slice the duck breasts and pour some sauce around each one, then garnish with slices of plum and chopped coriander.

Turkey with Fig, Orange and Mint Marmalade

Turkey is a low-fat meat that should be used all the year round, not just at Christmas. This unusual sauce gives its rather bland flavour a tremendous lift.

SERVES 4

500 g/1 lb dried figs

½ bottle sweet, fruity white wine

4 turkey fillets, 170-225 g/6-8 oz each

1 tbsp butter

2 tbsp dark orange marmalade

10 mint leaves, finely chopped, plus a few more to garnish

juice of ½ lemon

salt and pepper

1 Place the figs in a pan with the wine and bring to the boil, then simmer very gently for about 1 hour. Leave to cool and refrigerate overnight.

2 Melt the butter in a pan and fry the turkey fillets until they are cooked through. Remove from the pan and keep warm. Drain any fat from the pan and pour in the juice from the figs. Bring to the boil and reduce until about 150 ml/¼ pint/⅔ cup remains.

3 Add the marmalade, mint leaves and lemon juice, and simmer for a few minutes. Season to taste. When the sauce is thick and shiny, pour it over the meat and garnish with the figs and mint leaves.

Lamb with Mint and Lemon

Lamb has been served with mint for many years – rightly, because it is a great combination.

SERVES 8

8 lamb steaks, 225 g/8 oz each

grated rind and juice of 1 lemon

2 cloves garlic, peeled and crushed

2 spring onions, finely chopped

2 tsp finely chopped fresh mint leaves, plus some leaves for garnishing

4 tbsp extra virgin olive oil

salt and black pepper

1 Make a marinade for the lamb by mixing all the other ingredients and seasoning to taste. Place the lamb steaks in a shallow dish and cover with the marinade. Refrigerate overnight.

2 Grill the lamb under a high heat until just cooked, basting with the marinade occasionally during cooking. Turn once during cooking. Garnish with mint leaves.

Sirloin Steaks with Bloody Mary Sauce and Coriander

This cocktail of ingredients is just as successful as the well-known drink, but the alcohol evaporates in cooking, so you need not worry about a hangover.

SERVES 4

4 sirloin steaks, 225 g/8 oz each
MARINADE
2 tbsp soy sauce
4 tbsp balsamic vinegar
2 tbsp olive oil
SAUCE
1 kg/2 lb very ripe tomatoes, peeled and chopped
tomato purée, if required
50 g/2 oz/½ cup chopped onions
2 spring onions
1 tsp chopped fresh coriander
1 tsp ground cumin
1 tsp salt
1 tbsp fresh lime juice
120 ml/4 fl oz/½ cup beef consommé
60 ml/2 fl oz/¼ cup vodka
1 tbsp Worcester sauce

1 Lay the steaks in a shallow dish, mix the marinade ingredients together in a bowl, pour over the steaks and leave for at least a couple of hours in the refrigerator, turning once or twice.

2 If the tomatoes are not quite ripe, add a little tomato purée. Place all the sauce ingredients in a food processor and blend to a fairly smooth texture. Put in a pan, bring to the boil and simmer for about 5 minutes.

3 Remove the steaks from the marinade and place under a hot grill. Discard the marinade. Grill the steaks under a high heat until cooked. Serve with the sauce.

Roast Pork with Sage, Marjoram and Celery Leaves

Pork is an inexpensive choice which is equally suitable for a family dinner or a celebration meal. The fruity purée makes a delicious change from the more usual plain apple sauce.

SERVES 8

2.75 kg/6 lb joint of pork
3 tbsp fresh sage
1 tbsp fresh marjoram
3 tbsp chopped celery leaves
salt and pepper
50 ml/2 fl oz/¼ cup cider
PURÉE
15 ml/1 tbsp butter
2 eating apples
2 bananas
1 tbsp Calvados

1 Preheat the oven to 165°C/315°F/gas 2½. Cut a large piece of foil and place the pork in the centre. In a bowl mix the sage, marjoram and celery leaves together. Cover the fatty part of the pork with the herb mixture, season to taste and wrap tightly. Roast for about 1 hour.

2 Fold back the foil and baste the joint with the cider. Continue cooking for another hour until a sharp knife pressed into the thickest part produces clear juices.

3 To make the purée, peel and slice the apples and bananas, put the butter in a pan and sauté the fruit. Add the Calvados and set it alight. When the flames have died down remove the mixture from the heat, put it in the food processor and purée. Serve the pork with the purée on the side.

From top: *Sirloin Steaks with Bloody Mary Sauce and Coriander; Roast Pork with Sage, Marjoram and Celery Leaves*

Sweetcorn in a Garlic Butter Crust

Whether you are catering for vegetarians or serving this with other meat dishes, it will disappear in a flash. Even people who are not usually keen on corn on the cob have been won over by this recipe.

SERVES 6

6 ripe cobs of corn

225 g/8 oz/1 cup butter

2 tbsp olive oil

2 cloves garlic, peeled and crushed

2 tsp freshly ground black pepper

115 g/4 oz/1 cup wholemeal breadcrumbs

1 tbsp chopped parsley

1 Boil the corn cobs in salted water until tender, then leave to cool.

2 Melt the butter, and add the oil, garlic and black pepper. Pour the mixture into a shallow dish. Mix the breadcrumbs and parsley in another shallow dish. Roll the corn cobs in the melted butter mixture and then in the breadcrumbs.

3 Grill the cobs under a high grill until the breadcrumbs are golden.

OTHER GARLIC BUTTER IDEAS

• Partially cut through a French loaf at regular intervals. Spread the garlic butter mixture between the slices and bake in a moderate oven for 30 minutes.

• To make garlic croutons, melt the garlic butter in a pan and add cubes of bread. Toss frequently over a medium heat. When golden brown add to soups or salads.

• Drizzle over chicken breasts before roasting.

Vegetable and Herb Kebabs with Green Peppercorn Sauce

Other vegetables can be included in these kebabs, depending on what is available at the time. The green peppercorn sauce is also an excellent accompaniment to many other dishes.

SERVES 4

8 bamboo skewers soaked in water for 1 hour
24 mushrooms
16 cherry tomatoes
16 large basil leaves
16 thick slices of courgette
16 large mint leaves
16 squares of red sweet pepper

TO BASTE
120 ml/4 fl oz/½ cup melted butter
1 clove garlic, peeled and crushed
1 tbsp crushed green peppercorns
salt
GREEN PEPPERCORN SAUCE
50 g/2 oz/¼ cup butter
3 tbsp brandy
250 ml/8 fl oz/1 cup double cream
1 tsp crushed green peppercorns

1 Thread the vegetables on to the bamboo skewers. Place the basil leaves immediately next to the tomatoes, and the mint leaves wrapped around the courgette slices.

2 Mix the basting ingredients and baste the kebabs thoroughly. Place the skewers on a barbecue or under the grill, turning and basting regularly until the vegetables are just cooked – about 5-7 minutes.

3 Heat the butter for the sauce in a frying pan, then add the brandy and light it. When the flames have died down, stir in the cream and the peppercorns. Cook for approximately 2 minutes, stirring all the time. Serve the kebabs with the green peppercorn sauce.

Garlic and Marjoram Mushrooms with Pumpkin Seed and Tomato Bread

Garlic mushrooms are always popular, and this unusual Italian-style bread makes a delicious accompaniment.

SERVES 6

GARLIC MUSHROOMS

350 g/12 oz mushrooms

3 tbsp olive oil

1 tbsp water

2 cloves garlic, peeled and crushed

4 tbsp chopped fresh marjoram

juice of 1 lemon

salt and pepper

TOMATO BREAD

50 g/2 oz/⅓ cup sun-dried tomatoes
    in olive oil

200 ml/7 fl oz/scant 1 cup boiling
    water

1 tsp chopped fresh basil

1 tsp chopped fresh marjoram

1 tsp chopped fresh rosemary

50 g/2 oz/generous 3 tbsp butter

1 tsp salt

500 g/1 lb/4 cups plain flour

1 sachet (7 g/¼ oz) dried yeast

3 tbsp olive oil

1 egg

1 tbsp pumpkin seeds

1 To cook the mushrooms, put all the ingredients in a saucepan and bring the liquid to the boil, then turn down the heat and simmer for 10 minutes. Tip the mushrooms and liquid into a bowl. Refrigerate overnight.

From top: *Chicken Drumsticks in a Honey and Coriander Crust; Garlic and Marjoram Mushrooms with Tomato Bread*

2 To make the bread, drain the tomatoes and chop roughly. Put them in a bowl and pour on the boiling water. Add the herbs and leave to soak for 20-25 minutes.

3 Place the butter, salt and flour in a mixing bowl and rub the fat into the flour until the mixture resembles breadcrumbs. Stir in the yeast. Drain the liquid from the tomatoes, reserving the liquid, and heat this until lukewarm. Add the drained tomatoes.

4 Mix the tomato and herb liquid with the olive oil and egg. Make a well in the centre of the flour mixture and pour in most of the liquid mixture. Mix well to form a fairly stiff dough. If it is too stiff, add more liquid.

5 Knead the dough until smooth, in the bowl or on a floured board or surface. Form into a round loaf shape and put this on a greased baking sheet. Cover with a clean cloth and leave in a warm room until slightly risen – this will take about 30 minutes. Preheat the oven to 220°C/425°F/gas 7.

6 Brush the loaf with a little water and gently press the pumpkin seeds into the top and sides. Bake for 15-20 minutes. Turn the loaf out on to a wire rack. Tap the upturned bottom. If the loaf is done it will sound hollow – if not, put it back in the oven for a few more minutes. Let it cool before slicing.

Chicken Drumsticks in a Honey and Coriander Crust

This delicious crunchy coating will be a hit with guests and family alike.

MAKES 8 DRUMSTICKS

8 chicken drumsticks

170 g/6 oz/¾ cup butter

2 tbsp sunflower oil

5 tbsp clear honey

1 tbsp French mustard

1 tsp roughly crushed coriander seeds

1 tsp freshly ground black pepper

450 g/1 lb/4 cups breadcrumbs

coriander sprigs, to garnish

1 Grill the chicken drumsticks for 6 minutes, turning several times. Place the butter, oil and honey in a small pan and warm until all three ingredients are combined.

2 Preheat the oven to 180°C/350°F/gas 4. Add the mustard, coriander and pepper to the mixture. Stir well and brush on to the chicken. Roll in the breadcrumbs.

3 Bake in the oven for 20-25 minutes until fully cooked through. When cooked, the juices should run clear. Serve garnished with a sprig of coriander.

Lamb Steaks Marinated in Mint and Sherry

The marinade is the key to the success of this recipe. The sherry imparts a wonderful tang.

SERVES 6

6 large lamb steaks or 12 smaller chops

MARINADE

2 tbsp chopped fresh mint leaves

1 tbsp black peppercorns

1 medium onion, chopped

120 ml/4 fl oz/½ cup sherry

60 ml/2 fl oz/¼ cup extra virgin olive oil

2 cloves garlic

1 Place the mint leaves and peppercorns in a food processor and blend until very finely chopped. Add the chopped onion and process again until smooth. Add the rest of the marinade ingredients and process until completely mixed. The marinade should be of a fairly thick consistency.

2 Place the steaks or chops in a shallow dish and pour on the marinade. Cover with non-PVC clear film and refrigerate overnight.

3 Grill or barbecue the steaks on a very high heat until cooked, basting occasionally with the marinade.

Salmon Steaks with Oregano Salsa

This combination of salmon with piquant tomato works incredibly well. An ideal dish for a summer lunch.

<u>Serves 4</u>

1 tbsp butter

4 salmon steaks, 225 g/8 oz each

120 ml/4 fl oz/½ cup white wine

½ tsp freshly ground black pepper

fresh oregano, to make 2 tsp
 chopped, plus sprigs to garnish

4 spring onions, trimmed

225 g/8 oz ripe tomatoes, peeled

2 tbsp extra virgin olive oil

½ tsp caster sugar

1 tbsp tomato purée

1 Preheat the oven to 140°C/275°F/ gas 1. Butter an ovenproof dish, put in the salmon steaks, and add the wine and black pepper. Cover with silver foil and bake for 15 minutes, until the fish is just cooked. Leave to cool.

2 Put the oregano in a food processor and chop it very finely. Add the spring onions, tomatoes and all the remaining ingredients. Process in bursts until chopped but not a smooth purée.

3 Serve the salmon cold with the salsa, garnished with a sprig of fresh oregano.

Guacamole, Basil and Tomato Pitta Breads

This is a favourite family recipe – the fresh basil and tomato are perfect partners for each other and for the spicy guacamole.

SERVES 6

6 large pitta breads
1-2 large beef tomatoes, sliced
12 basil leaves
2 large ripe avocados
1 tomato
½ red onion
1 clove garlic, peeled and crushed
1 tbsp lime juice
¼ tsp chilli powder
2 tbsp chopped fresh dill

1 Open the ends of the pitta breads to make pockets and place a couple of slices of tomato and two basil leaves in each one.

2 Roughly chop the avocados, the remaining tomato and the red onion. Mix all the remaining ingredients briefly in a food processor.

3 Add the mixture from the food processor to the roughly chopped avocado, tomato and onions, and stir gently. Fill the pockets with the avocado mixture and serve immediately.

Brie and Grape Sandwiches with Mint

A slightly unusual sandwich combination, which works well judging by the speed with which the sandwiches disappear at family picnics or summer tea parties.

SERVES 4

8 thick slices Granary bread
butter for spreading
350 g/12 oz ripe Brie cheese
30-40 large grapes
16 fresh mint leaves

1 Butter the bread. Slice the Brie into thick slices, to be divided between the sandwiches.

2 Place the Brie slices on four slices of bread. Peel, halve and seed the grapes and put on top of the Brie. Chop the mint finely by hand or in a food processor, and sprinkle the mint over the Brie and grapes. Place the other four slices of bread over the top and cut each sandwich in half.

OTHER HERB SANDWICH IDEAS

- Feta cheese, black olives, lettuce, tomato and freshly chopped mint in pitta bread
- Italian salami, cream cheese, tomato and fresh basil on ciabatta bread
- Sliced chicken breast, mayonnaise and dill sprigs on granary bread
- Grilled mozzarella and sun-dried tomato foccaccia bread sandwich, with black olives, fresh rocket and basil leaves
- Hummus, lettuce and freshly chopped coriander on French bread
- Dry cured Parma ham, green olives and rocket leaves on poppy-seeded white bread

From top: *Brie and Grape Sandwiches with Mint; Guacamole, Basil and Tomato Pitta Breads*

Broccoli and Cauliflower with a Cider and Apple Mint Sauce

The cider sauce made here is also ideal for other vegetables, such as celery or beans. It is flavoured using tamari, a Japanese soy sauce and apple mint.

S<small>ERVES</small> 4

1 large onion, chopped

2 large carrots, chopped

1 large clove garlic

1 tbsp dill seed

4 large sprigs apple mint

2 tbsp olive oil

2 tbsp plain flour

300 ml/½ pint/1¼ cups dry cider

500 g/1 lb broccoli florets

500 g/1 lb cauliflower florets

2 tbsp tamari

2 tsp mint jelly

1 Sauté the onions, carrots, garlic, dill seeds and apple mint leaves in the olive oil until nearly cooked. Stir in the flour and cook for half a minute or so. Pour in the cider and simmer until the sauce looks glossy.

2 Boil the broccoli and cauliflower in separate pans until tender.

3 Pour the sauce into a food processor and add the tamari and the mint jelly. Blend until finely puréed. Pour over the broccoli and cauliflower.

Courgette and Carrot Ribbons with Brie, Black Pepper and Parsley

This recipe produces a delicious vegetarian meal, or simply a new way of presenting colourful vegetables as an accompaniment to a main course.

SERVES 4

1 large green pepper, diced

1 tbsp sunflower oil

225 g/8 oz Brie cheese

2 tbsp crème fraîche

1 tsp lemon juice

4 tbsp milk

2 tsp freshly ground black pepper

2 tbsp parsley, very finely chopped,
   plus extra to garnish

salt and pepper

6 large courgettes

6 large carrots

1 Sauté the green pepper in the sunflower oil until just tender. Place the remaining ingredients, apart from the carrots and courgettes, in a food processor and blend well. Place the mixture in a saucepan and add the green pepper.

2 Peel the courgettes. Use a potato peeler to slice them into long, thin strips. Do the same thing with the carrots. Put the courgettes and carrots in separate saucepans, cover with just enough water to cover, then simmer for 3 minutes until barely cooked.

3 Heat the sauce and pour into a shallow vegetable dish. Toss the courgette and carrot strips together and arrange them in the sauce. Garnish with a little finely chopped parsley.

Smoked Salmon, Lemon and Dill Pasta

This has been tried and tested as both a main-dish salad and a starter, and the only preference stated was that as a main dish you got a larger portion, so that made it better.

SERVES 2 AS A MAIN COURSE OR 4 AS A STARTER

salt
350 g/12 oz/3 cups pasta twists
6 large sprigs fresh dill, chopped,
 plus more sprigs to garnish
2 tbsp extra virgin olive oil
1 tbsp white wine vinegar
300 ml/½ pint/1¼ cups double cream
pepper
170 g/6 oz smoked salmon

1 Boil the pasta in salted water until it is just cooked. Drain and run under the cold tap until completely cooled.

2 Make the dressing by combining all the remaining ingredients, apart from the smoked salmon and reserved dill, in the bowl of a food processor and blend well. Season to taste.

3 Slice the salmon into small strips. Place the cooled pasta and the smoked salmon, in a mixing bowl. Pour on the dressing and toss carefully. Transfer to a serving bowl and garnish with the dill sprigs.

Avocado and Pasta Salad with Coriander

Served as one of a variety of salads or alone, this tasty combination is sure to please. The dressing is fairly sharp, yet tastes wonderfully fresh.

SERVES 4

115 g/4 oz/1¼ cups pasta shells or
 bows
900 ml/1½ pints/3¾ cups chicken stock
4 sticks celery, finely chopped
2 avocados, chopped
1 clove garlic, peeled and chopped
1 tbsp finely chopped fresh coriander,
 plus some whole leaves to garnish
115 g/4 oz/1 cup grated mature
 Cheddar cheese
DRESSING
150 ml/¼ pint/⅔ cup extra virgin
 olive oil
1 tbsp cider vinegar
2 tbsp lemon juice
grated rind of 1 lemon
1 tsp French mustard
1 tbsp chopped fresh coriander
salt and pepper

1 Bring the chicken stock to the boil, add the pasta, and simmer for about 10 minutes until just cooked. Drain and cool under cold running water.

2 Mix the celery, avocados, garlic and chopped coriander in a bowl and add the cooled pasta. Sprinkle with the grated Cheddar.

3 To make the dressing place all the ingredients in a food processor and process until the coriander is finely chopped. Serve separately, or pour over the salad and toss before serving. Garnish with coriander leaves.

From top: *Smoked Salmon, Lemon and Dill Pasta; Avocado and Pasta Salad with Coriander*

Stuffed Tomatoes, with Wild Rice, Corn and Coriander

 These tomatoes could be served as a light meal with crusty bread and a salad, or as an accompaniment to most meats or fish.

SERVES 4

8 medium tomatoes

50 g/2 oz/⅓ cup sweetcorn kernels

2 tbsp white wine

50 g/2 oz/¼ cup cooked wild rice

1 clove garlic

50 g/2 oz/½ cup grated Cheddar cheese

1 tbsp chopped fresh coriander

salt and pepper

1 tbsp olive oil

1 Cut the tops off the tomatoes and remove the seeds with a small teaspoon. Scoop out all the flesh and chop finely – also chop the tops.

2 Preheat the oven to 180°C/350°F/gas 4. Put the chopped tomato in a pan. Add the sweetcorn and the white wine. Cover with a close-fitting lid and simmer until tender. Drain.

3 Mix together all the remaining ingredients except the olive oil, adding salt and pepper to taste. Carefully spoon the mixture into the tomatoes, piling it higher in the centre. Sprinkle the oil over the top, arrange the tomatoes in an ovenproof dish, and bake at 180°C/350°F/gas 4 for 15-20 minutes until cooked through.

Spinach, Walnut and Gruyère Lasagne with Basil

This nutty lasagne is a delicious combination of flavours which easily equals the traditional meat and tomato version.

SERVES 8

350 g/12 oz spinach lasagne (quick cooking)

WALNUT AND TOMATO SAUCE

3 tbsp walnut oil

1 large onion, chopped

225 g/8 oz celeriac, finely chopped

1 x 400 g/14 oz can chopped tomatoes

1 large clove garlic, finely chopped

½ tsp sugar

115 g/4 oz/²⁄₃ cup chopped walnuts

150 ml/¼ pint/²⁄₃ cup Dubonnet

SPINACH AND GRUYERE SAUCE

75 g/3 oz/⅓ cup butter

2 tbsp walnut oil

1 medium onion, chopped

75 g/3 oz/²⁄₃ cup flour

1 tsp mustard powder

1.2 litres/2 pints/5 cups milk

225 g/8 oz/2 cups grated Gruyère cheese

salt and pepper

ground nutmeg

500 g/1 lb frozen spinach, thawed and puréed

2 tbsp basil, chopped

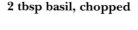

1 First make the walnut and tomato sauce. Heat the walnut oil and sauté the onion and celeriac. Cook for about 8-10 minutes. Meanwhile purée the tomatoes in a food processor. Add the garlic to the pan and cook for about 1 minute, then add the sugar, walnuts, tomatoes and Dubonnet. Season to taste. Simmer, uncovered, for 25 minutes.

2 To make the spinach and Gruyère sauce, melt the butter with the walnut oil and add the onion. Cook for 5 minutes, then stir in the flour. Cook for another minute and add the mustard powder and milk, stirring vigorously. When the sauce has come to the boil,

take off the heat and add three-quarters of the grated Gruyère. Season to taste with salt, pepper and nutmeg. Finally add the puréed spinach.

3 Preheat the oven to 180°C/350°F/gas 4. Layer the lasagne in an ovenproof dish. Start with a layer of the spinach and Gruyère sauce, then add a little walnut and tomato sauce, then a layer of lasagne, and continue until the dish is full, ending with layer of either sauce.

4 Sprinkle the remaining Gruyère over the top of the dish, followed by the basil. Bake for 45 minutes.

Potato Salad with Curry Plant Mayonnaise

Potato salad can be made well in advance and is therefore a useful buffet dish. Its popularity means that there are very rarely any leftovers.

Serves 6

salt

1 kg/2 lb new potatoes, in skins

300 ml/½ pint/1¼ cups shop-bought mayonnaise

6 curry plant leaves, roughly chopped

black pepper

mixed lettuce or other salad greens, to serve

1 Place the potatoes in a pan of salted water and boil for 15 minutes or until tender. Drain and place in a large bowl to cool slightly.

2 Mix the mayonnaise with the curry plant leaves and black pepper. Stir these into the potatoes while they are still warm. Leave to cool, then serve on a bed of mixed lettuce or other assorted salad leaves.

Tomato, Savory and French Bean Salad

Savory and beans must have been invented for each other. This salad mixes them with ripe tomatoes, making a superb accompaniment for all cold meats or vegetable salads.

Serves 4

500 g/1 lb French beans

1 kg/2 lb ripe tomatoes

3 spring onions, roughly sliced

1 tbsp pine nuts

4 sprigs fresh savory

For the dressing

2 tbsp extra virgin olive oil

juice of 1 lime

75 g/3 oz Dolcelatte cheese

1 clove garlic, peeled and crushed

salt and pepper

1 Prepare the dressing first so that it can stand a while before using. Place all the dressing ingredients in the bowl of a food processor, season to taste and blend until all the cheese has been finely chopped and you have a smooth dressing. Pour it into a jug.

2 Top and tail the beans, and boil in salted water until they are just cooked. Drain them and run cold water over them until they have completely cooled. Slice the tomatoes, or, if they are fairly small, quarter them.

3 Toss the salad ingredients together, except for the pine nuts and savory. Pour on the salad dressing. Sprinkle the pine nuts over the top, followed by the savory.

Summer Fruit Gâteau with Heartsease

No one could resist the appeal of little heartsease pansies. This cake would be lovely for a sentimental summer occasion in the garden.

SERVES 6-8

100 g/3¾ oz/scant ½ cup soft margarine, plus more to grease mould
100 g/3¾ oz/scant ½ cup sugar
2 tsp clear honey
150 g/5 oz/1¼ cups self-raising flour
½ tsp baking powder
2 tbsp milk
2 eggs, plus white of one more for crystallizing
1 tbsp rosewater
1 tbsp Cointreau
16 heartsease pansy flowers
caster sugar, as required, to crystallize
icing sugar, to decorate
500 g/1 lb strawberries
strawberry leaves, to decorate

1 Preheat the oven to 190°C/375°F/ gas 5. Grease and lightly flour a ring mould. Take a large mixing bowl and add the soft margarine, sugar, honey, flour, baking powder, milk and 2 eggs to the mixing bowl and beat well for 1 minute. Add the rosewater and the Cointreau and mix well.

2 Pour the mixture into the tin and bake for 40 minutes. Allow to stand for a few minutes and then turn out onto the plate that you wish to serve it on.

3 Crystallize the heartsease pansies, by painting them with lightly beaten egg white and sprinkling with caster sugar. Leave to dry.

4 Sift icing sugar over the cake. Fill the centre of the ring with strawberries – if they will not all fit, place some around the edge. Decorate with crystallized heartsease flowers and some strawberry leaves.

Borage, Mint and Lemon Balm Sorbet

Borage has such a pretty flower head that it is worth growing just to make this recipe, and to float the flowers in summer drinks. The sorbet itself has a very refreshing, delicate taste, perfect for a hot afternoon.

SERVES 6-8

500 g/1 lb/2⅛ cups sugar
500 ml/17 fl oz/2⅛ cups water
6 sprigs mint, plus more to decorate
6 lemon balm leaves
250 ml/8 fl oz/1 cup white wine
2 tbsp lemon juice
borage sprigs, to decorate

1 Place the sugar and water in a saucepan with the washed herbs. Bring to the boil. Remove from the heat and add the wine. Cover and cool. Chill for several hours, then add the lemon juice. Freeze in a suitable container. As soon as the mixture begins to freeze, stir it briskly and replace in the freezer. Repeat every 15 minutes for at least 3 hours or until ready to serve.

2 To make the small ice bowls, pour about 1 cm/½ in cold, boiled water into small freezer-proof bowls, about 600 ml/1 pint/1¼ US pints in capacity, and arrange some herbs in the water. Place in the freezer. Once this has frozen add a little more water to cover the herbs and freeze.

3 Place a smaller freezer-proof bowl inside the larger bowl and put a heavy weight inside such as a metal weight from some scales. Fill with more cooled boiled water, float more herbs in this and freeze.

4 To release the ice bowls, warm the inner bowl with a small amount of very hot water and twist it out. Warm the outer bowl by standing it in very hot water for a few seconds, then tip out the ice bowl. Spoon the sorbet into the ice bowls, decorate with sprigs of mint and borage and serve.

From top: *Summer Fruit Gateau; Borage, Mint and Lemon Balm Sorbet*

Lemon Meringue Bombe with Mint Chocolate

This easy ice cream will cause a sensation at a dinner party – it is unusual but quite the most delicious combination of tastes that you can imagine.

SERVES 6-8

2 large lemons

150 g/5 oz/²⁄₃ cup granulated sugar

3 small sprigs fresh mint

150 ml/¹⁄₄ pint/²⁄₃ cup whipping cream

600 ml/1 pint/2¹⁄₂ cups Greek natural yogurt

2 large meringues

225 g/8 oz good-quality mint chocolate, grated

1 Slice the rind off the lemons with a potato peeler, then squeeze them for juice. Place the lemon rind and sugar in a food processor and blend finely. Add the cream, yoghurt and lemon juice and process thoroughly. Pour the mixture into a mixing bowl and add the meringues, roughly crushed.

2 Reserve one of the mint sprigs and chop the rest finely. Add to the cream and lemon mixture. Pour into a 1.2 litre/2 pint/1¹⁄₄ US quart glass pudding basin and freeze for 4 hours.

3 When the ice cream has frozen, scoop out the middle and pour in the grated mint chocolate, reserving a little for the garnish. Replace the ice cream to cover the chocolate and refreeze.

4 To turn out, dip the basin in very hot water for a few seconds to loosen the ice cream, then turn the basin upside down over the serving plate. Decorate with grated chocolate and a sprig of mint.

Apple Mint and Pink Grapefruit Fool

Apple mint can easily run riot in the herb garden; this is an excellent way of using up an abundant crop.

SERVES 4-6

500 g/1 lb tart apples, peeled and sliced

225 g/8 oz pink grapefruit segments

3 tbsp clear honey

2 tbsp water

6 large sprigs apple mint, plus more to garnish

150 ml/¼ pint/⅔ cup double cream

300 ml/½ pint/1¼ cups custard

1 Place the apples, grapefruit, honey, water and apple mint in a pan, cover and simmer for 10 minutes until soft. Leave in the pan to cool, then discard the apple mint. Purée the mixture in a food processor.

2 Whip the double cream until it forms soft peaks, and fold into the custard, keeping 2 tablespoonfuls to decorate. Carefully fold the cream into the apple and grapefruit mixture. Serve in individual glasses, chilled and decorated with swirls of cream and small sprigs of apple mint.

Passion Fruit and Angelica Syllabub

Passion fruit have a unique fragrance and flavour which makes this syllabub quite irresistible.

SERVES 6

6 passion fruit

1 tbsp chopped crystallized angelica, plus more to decorate

grated rind and juice of 2 limes

120 ml/4 fl oz/½ cup white wine

50 g/2 oz/⅓ cup icing sugar

300 ml/½ pint/1¼ cups double cream

150 ml/¼ pint/⅔ cup Greek natural yogurt

1 Scoop out the flesh, seeds and juice of the passion fruit and divide between 6 serving dishes. Place the crystallized angelica in a food processor with the lime rind and juice, and blend to a purée.

2 In a large bowl, mix the lime pureé with the wine and icing sugar. Stir until the sugar is dissolved.

3 Whip the double cream until it begins to form soft peaks and then gradually beat in the wine mixture – the cream should thicken slightly. Whisk in the yogurt.

4 Spoon the cream mixture over the passion fruit, and refrigerate until ready to serve. Decorate with more crystallized angelica before serving.

Japanese Fruit Salad with Mint and Coffee

This dessert was served in a Japanese department store. Although it sounds a little strange, it works very well — the coffee flavour is excellent with the fruit.

SERVES 6

12 canned lychees and the juice from the can

1 small fresh pineapple

2 large ripe pears

2 fresh peaches

12 strawberries

6 small sprigs of mint plus 12 extra sprigs to decorate

1 tbsp instant coffee granules

2 tbsp boiling water

150 ml/¼ pint/⅔ cup double cream

1 Peel the fruit as necessary and chop into equal-sized pieces. Place all the fruit in a large glass bowl and pour on the lychee juice.

2 Put the mint, coffee granules and boiling water in a food processor. Blend until smooth. Add the cream and process again briefly.

3 Serve the fruit salad drained and chilled, with two small sprigs of mint on each plate, and the coffee sauce separately.

Clementines in Beaumes de Venise with Geranium

The fantastic bonus of using this recipe is that you have half a bottle of Beaumes de Venise left over, which simply has to be drunk as a digestif.

SERVES 6

10 whole clementines
12 scented geranium leaves
¹/₂ bottle Muscat de Beaumes de Venise
orange leaves, to decorate

1 Peel the clementines and remove the pith.

2 Place the clementines in a glass dish and pour over the wine. Add the scented geranium leaves and refrigerate overnight. Discard leaves, then serve chilled and decorated with orange leaves. Any juice left over from this dessert can be served as a *digestif*.

Chocolate Mint Truffle Filo Parcels

These exquisite little parcels are utterly irresistible. There will be no leftovers.

18 PARCELS

1 tbsp very finely chopped mint

75 g/3 oz/¾ cup ground almonds

50 g/2 oz plain chocolate, grated

2 dessert apples, peeled and grated

115 g/4 oz crème fraîche or fromage frais

9 large sheets filo pastry

75 g/3 oz/⅓ cup butter, melted

1 tbsp icing sugar, to dust

1 tbsp cocoa powder, to dust

1 Preheat the oven to 190°C/375°F/ gas 5. Mix the mint, almonds, chocolate, crème fraîche and grated apple in a bowl. Cut the filo pastry sheets into 7.5 cm/3 in squares, and cover with a cloth to prevent them from drying out.

2 Brush a square of filo with melted butter, lay on a second sheet, brush again, and place a spoonful of filling in the middle of the top sheet. Bring in all four corners and twist to form a purse shape. Repeat to make 18 parcels.

3 Place the filo parcels on a baking sheet, well brushed with melted butter. Bake for approximately 10 minutes. Leave to cool and then dust with the icing sugar, and then with the cocoa powder.

From left to right: *Clementines in Beaumes de Venise with Geranium; Chocolate Mint Truffle Filo Parcels*

Rosemary Vinegar

Flavoured vinegars make a huge difference to the taste of a salad dressing. They are very simple to make, and the jars are a pretty window-sill decoration. Try the same recipe with nasturtium flowers, if you like.

ABOUT 600 ML/1 PINT/2½ CUPS

rosemary sprigs, to fill a 600 ml/1 pint/2½ cup measure, plus more to decorate

600 ml/1 pint/2½ cups white distilled vinegar

1 Fill a sterilized wide-necked bottle or jar with the sprigs of rosemary. Fill to the top with vinegar. Cover tightly and place in a sunny spot for around 4-6 weeks.

2 Filter the vinegar mixture through a coffee filter paper. Discard the rosemary. Heat the vinegar until it begins to simmer, but do not boil.

3 Wash the bottle or jar and its lid well in hot, soapy water, rinse thoroughly, and dry in a warm oven. Pour the vinegar back into it or other sterilized decorative bottles. You can add a fresh sprig or two of rosemary for decorative purposes if you wish, then seal. Store in a dark place. Use within one year.

Herb Garden Dressing

 *This dried mixture will keep through the winter until your herbs are growing again. It can be used to flavour salad dressings and to sprinkle over vegetables, casseroles and stews.*

115 g/4 oz/1 cup dried oregano
115 g/4 oz/1 cup dried basil
50 g/2 oz/½ cup dried marjoram
50 g/2 oz/½ cup dried dill weed
50 g/2 oz/½ cup dried mint leaves
50 g/2 oz/½ cup onion powder
2 tbsp dry mustard
2 tsp salt
1 tbsp freshly ground black pepper

1 Mix the ingredients together and keep in a sealed jar to use as needed.

2 When making a batch of salad dressing, take 2 tbsp of the herb mixture and add it to 350 ml/ 12 fl oz/1½ cups of extra virgin olive oil and 120 ml/4 fl oz/½ cup cider vinegar. Mix thoroughly and allow to stand for 1 hour or so. Mix again before using.

Dill Pickles

A good pickle to have in your store cupboard. It is excellent sliced into hamburger, served with cold meats, and in canapés and snacks. If you like, try varying the type of cucumbers used. The French are fond of tiny 'cornichons', while the traditional Northern and Eastern European gherkins are much larger.

ABOUT 2.5 LITRES/4 PINTS/2½ US QUARTS

6 small cucumbers

400 ml/16 fl oz/2 cups water

1 litre/1¾ pints/4 cups white wine vinegar

115 g/4 oz/½ cup salt

3 bay leaves

3 tbsp dill seed

2 cloves garlic, slivered

dill flowerheads, to garnish

1 Slice the cucumbers into medium-thick slices. Put the water, vinegar and salt in a saucepan and boil, then remove immediately from the heat.

2 Layer the herbs and garlic between slices of cucumber in sterilized preserving jars until the jars are full, then cover with the warm salt and vinegar mixture. Leave on a sunny window sill for at least a week before using.

Parsley, Sage and Thyme Oil

Herb oils are an excellent ingredient for use in stir-fry cooking as well as salad dressings. This mixed herb combination is a good basic choice, but you can also be adventurous and try other, more exotic ingredients. Adding garlic and chillis to a herb oil produces a fiery condiment: try dribbling a tiny amount on to pasta for extra flavour.

600 ML/1 PINT/2½ CUPS

600 ml/1 pint/2½ cups sunflower oil

50 g/2 oz/½ cup chopped fresh parsley

25 g/1 oz/⅛ cup chopped fresh sage

50 g/2 oz/¼ cup chopped fresh thyme

1 Pour the oil into a sterilized jar and add all the herbs. Cover and allow to stand at room temperature for about a week, no longer. Stir or shake occasionally during that time.

2 Then strain off the oil into a sterilized bottle and discard the used herbs. Add a fresh sprig or two for decorative purposes if you wish. Seal the jar carefully. Store, preferably in a cool place, for 6 months at the most.

Cranberry and Port Sauce with Lemon Thyme

Cranberry and port sauce is delicious served with turkey, chicken, pork or ham. Lemon thyme really sets off its unique flavour.

ABOUT 600 ML/1 PINT/2½ CUPS

4 tbsp port
4 tbsp orange juice
115 g/4 oz/½ cup sugar
225 g/8 oz fresh cranberries
1 tbsp finely grated orange rind
1 tbsp very finely chopped lemon thyme

1 Pour the port and orange juice into a saucepan and add the sugar. Place the pan over a low heat and stir frequently with a metal spoon to dissolve the sugar.

2 Transfer the mixture to a larger pan. Increase the heat a little and add the cranberries. Bring the mixture to the boil and simmer for 5 minutes, stirring occasionally, until the cranberries are just tender and the skins begin to burst.

3 Remove the pan from the heat and carefully mix in the orange rind and lemon thyme.

4 Leave the sauce to cool, then pour into sterilized glass jars and seal with waxed paper circles and cellophane lids secured with rubber bands. Add a label and decorate with short lengths of string tied around the top if you like.

Lemon and Mint Curd

Home-made lemon curd is infinitely tastier than the commercial variety. The addition of mint gives this version an interesting extra tang. Try experimenting with different types of mint. Lemon curd is best made using the freshest of ingredients. Buy fresh eggs, and try to find unwaxed lemons.

ABOUT 1.5 KG/3 LB

6 fresh mint leaves
2 lb/900 g/4 cups caster sugar
350 g/12 oz/1½ cups butter, cut into chunks
rind of 6 lemons, thinly pared, in large pieces, and their juice
8 eggs, beaten

1 Place the mint leaves and sugar in a food processor, and blend until the mint leaves are very finely chopped and combined with the sugar.

2 Put the mint sugar and all the other ingredients into a bowl and mix together.

3 Set the bowl over a pan of simmering water. Cook, whisking gently, until all the butter has melted and the sugar has dissolved. Remove the lemon rind.

4 Continue to cook in this way, stirring frequently, for 35-40 minutes or until the mixture thickens. Pour into sterilized glass jars, filling them up to the rim. Seal with waxed paper circles and cellophane lids secured with rubber bands. Add a label and tie short lengths of string around the top of the jars to decorate. This lemon curd should be used within 3 months.

From top: *Lemon and Mint Curd; Cranberry and Port Sauce with Lemon Thyme*

Rhubarb and Ginger Mint Preserve

Ginger mint is easily grown in the garden, and is just the thing to boost the flavour of rhubarb jam. Stewed rhubarb also tastes good with a little ginger mint added to the pan.

ABOUT 2.75 KG/6 LB

2 kg/4 lb rhubarb

250 ml/8 fl oz/1 cup water

juice of 1 lemon

5 cm/2 in piece fresh root ginger, peeled

1.5 kg/3 lb/6 cups sugar

115 g/4 oz/²/₃ cup preserved stem ginger, chopped

2-3 tbsp very finely chopped ginger mint leaves

1 Wash and trim the rhubarb, cutting it into small pieces about 2.5 cm/1 in long. Place the rhubarb, water and lemon juice in a preserving pan and bring to the boil. Peel and bruise the piece of fresh root ginger and add it to the pan. Simmer, stirring frequently, until the rhubarb is soft and then remove the ginger.

2 Add the sugar and stir until it has dissolved. Bring the mixture to the boil and boil rapidly for 10-15 minutes, or until setting point is reached. With a metal slotted spoon, remove any scum from the surface of the jam.

3 Add the stem ginger and ginger mint leaves. Pour into sterilized glass jars, seal with waxed paper circles and cover with cellophane lids secured with rubber bands. Decorate with brown paper raffia.

Rose Petal Jelly

This subtle jelly is ideal for polite afternoon teas with thinly sliced pieces of bread and butter – it adds a real summer afternoon flavour to the bread.

ABOUT 900 G/2 LB

600 ml/1 pint/2½ cups red or pink rose petals

450 ml/³⁄₄ pint/1⁷⁄₈ cups water

700 g/1 lb 9 oz/generous 3 cups caster sugar

100 ml/3½ fl oz/scant ½ cup white grape juice

100 ml/3½ fl oz/scant ½ cup red grape juice

50 g/2 oz packet powdered fruit pectin

2 tbsp rosewater

1 Trim all the rose petals at the base to remove the white tips. Place the petals, water and about one-eighth of the sugar in a saucepan and bring to the boil. Reduce the heat and simmer for 5 minutes. Remove from the heat and leave to stand overnight for the rose fragrance to infuse.

2 Strain the flowers from the syrup, and put the syrup in a preserving pan or suitable saucepan. Add the grape juices and pectin. Boil hard for 1 minute. Add the rest of the sugar and stir well. Boil the mixture hard for 1 minute more. Remove from the heat.

3 Test for setting – it should make a soft jelly, not a thick jam. Do this by placing a teaspoonful of the hot mixture on a saucer. Leave it to cool: the surface should wrinkle when pushed with a finger. If it is still runny, return the pan to the heat and continue boiling and testing until the jelly sets.

4 Finally add the rosewater. Ladle the jelly into sterilized glass jars and seal with waxed paper circles and cellophane lids secured with rubber bands. Decorate the tops of the jars with circles of fabric held in place with lengths of ribbon.

Cheese and Marjoram Scones

A great success for a hearty tea. With savoury toppings, these scones can make a good basis for a light lunch, served with a crunchy, green salad.

ABOUT 18 SCONES

115 g/4 oz/1 cup wholemeal flour

115 g/4 oz/1 cup self-raising flour

pinch salt

40 g/1½ oz/scant 3 tbsp butter

¼ tsp dry mustard

2 tsp dried marjoram

50-75 g/2-3 oz/½-⅔ cup finely grated Cheddar cheese

1 tsp sunflower oil (optional)

120 ml/4 fl oz/½ cup milk, or as required

50 g/2 oz/⅓ cup pecan nuts or walnuts, chopped

1 Gently sift the two kinds of flour into a bowl and add the salt. Cut the butter into small pieces, and rub these into the flour until it resembles fine breadcrumbs.

2 Add the mustard, marjoram and grated cheese, and mix in sufficient milk to make a soft dough. Knead the dough lightly.

3 Preheat the oven to 220°C/425°F/gas 7. Roll out the dough on a floured surface to about 2 cm/¾ in thickness and cut it out with a 5 cm/2 in square cutter. Grease some baking trays with the paper from the butter (or use a little sunflower oil), and place the scones on the trays.

4 Brush the scones with a little milk and sprinkle the chopped pecans or walnuts over the top. Bake for 12 minutes. Serve warm.

Dill and Potato Cakes

Potato cakes are quite scrumptious and should be more widely made. Try this spendid combination and you are sure to be converted.

ABOUT 10 CAKES

225 g/8 oz/2 cups self-raising flour

3 tbsp butter, softened

pinch of salt

1 tbsp finely chopped fresh dill

170 g/6 oz/scant 1 cup mashed potato, freshly made

2-3 tbsp milk, as required

1 Preheat the oven to 230°C/450°F/ gas 8. Sift the flour into a bowl, and add the butter, salt and dill. Mix in the mashed potato and enough milk to make a soft, pliable dough.

2 Roll out the dough on a well-floured surface until it is fairly thin. Cut into neat rounds with a 7.5 cm/3 in cutter.

3 Grease a baking tray, place the cakes on it, and bake for 20-25 minutes until risen and golden.

Rosemary Bread

Sliced thinly, this herb bread is delicious with cheese or soup for a light meal.

1 LOAF

1 packet (7 g/¼ oz) dried fast-action yeast

170 g/6 oz/1½ cups wholemeal flour

170 g/6 oz/1½ cups self-raising flour

2 tbsp butter, plus more to grease bowl and tin

60 ml/2 fl oz/¼ cup warm water (45°C/110°F)

250 ml/8 fl oz/1 cup milk (room temperature)

1 tbsp sugar

1 tsp salt

1 tbsp sesame seeds

1 tbsp dried chopped onion

1 tbsp fresh rosemary leaves, plus more to decorate

115 g/4 oz/1 cup cubed Cheddar cheese

coarse salt, to decorate

1 Mix the fast-action yeast with the flours in a large mixing bowl. Melt the butter. Stir in the warm water, milk, sugar, butter, salt, sesame seeds, onion and rosemary. Knead thoroughly until quite smooth.

2 Flatten the dough, then add the cheese cubes. Quickly knead them in until they have been well combined.

3 Place the dough into a clean bowl greased with a little butter, turning it so that it becomes greased on all sides. Cover with a clean, dry cloth. Put the greased bowl and dough in a warm place for about 1½ hours, or until the dough has risen and doubled in size.

4 Grease a 23 x 13 cm/9 x 5 in loaf tin with the remaining butter. Knock down the dough to remove some of the air, and shape it into a loaf. Put the loaf into the tin, cover with the clean cloth used earlier and leave for about 1 hour until doubled in size once again. Preheat the oven to 190°C/ 375°F/gas 5.

5 Bake for 30 minutes. During the last 5-10 minutes of baking, cover the loaf with silver foil to prevent it from becoming too dark. Remove from the loaf tin and leave to cool on a wire rack. Decorate with rosemary leaves and coarse salt scattered on top.

Blackberry, Sloe Gin and Rosewater Muffins

Other berries can be substituted for the blackberries, such as elderberries or blueberries.

ABOUT 12 MUFFINS

300 g/11 oz/2½ cups plain white flour

50 g/2 oz/generous ¼ cup light brown sugar

4 tsp baking powder

pinch of salt

60 g/2¼ oz/generous ½ cup chopped blanched almonds

90 g/3½ oz/generous ½ cup fresh blackberries

2 eggs

200 ml/7 fl oz/⅞ cup milk

4 tbsp melted butter, plus a little more to grease cups, if using

1 tbsp sloe gin

1 tbsp rosewater

1 Mix the flour, sugar, baking powder and salt in a bowl and stir in the almonds and blackberries, mixing them well to coat with the flour mixture. Preheat the oven to 200°C/400°F/gas 6.

2 In another bowl, mix the eggs with the milk, then gradually add the butter, sloe gin and rosewater. Make a well in the centre of the bowl of dry ingredients and add the egg and milk mixture. Stir well.

3 Spoon the mixture into greased muffin cups or cases. Bake for 20-25 minutes or until browned. Turn out the muffins on to a wire rack to cool. Serve with butter.

Chocolate and Mint Fudge Cake

Chocolate and mint are popular partners and they blend well in this unusual recipe. The French have been using potato flour in cakes for years. Mashed potato works just as well.

1 CAKE

6-10 fresh mint leaves
170 g/6 oz/³⁄₄ cup caster sugar
115 g/4 oz/¹⁄₂ cup butter, plus extra to grease tin
75 g/3 oz/¹⁄₂ cup freshly made mashed potato
50 g/2 oz plain chocolate, melted
170 g/6 oz/1¹⁄₂ cups self-raising flour
pinch of salt
2 eggs, beaten
FILLING
4 fresh mint leaves
115 g/4 oz/¹⁄₂ cup butter
115 g/4 oz/⁷⁄₈ cup icing sugar
2 tbsp chocolate mint liqueur
TOPPING
225 g/8 oz/1 cup butter
50 g/2 oz/¹⁄₄ cup granulated sugar
2 tbsp chocolate mint liqueur
2 tbsp water
170 g/6 oz/1¹⁄₂ cups icing sugar
25 g/1 oz/¹⁄₄ cup cocoa powder
pecan halves, to decorate

1 Tear the mint leaves into small pieces and mix with the caster sugar. Leave overnight. When you use the flavoured sugar, remove the leaves and discard them.

Opposite: *Chocolate and Mint Fudge Cake; Strawberry Mint Sponge*

2 Preheat the oven to 200°C/400°F/gas 6. Cream the butter and sugar with the mashed potato, then add the melted chocolate. Sift in half the flour with a pinch of salt and add half of the beaten eggs. Mix well, then add the remaining flour and eggs.

3 Grease and line a 20 cm/8 in tin and pile in the mixture. Bake for 25-30 minutes or until a skewer or pointed knife stuck into the centre comes away clean. Turn out on to a wire rack to cool. When cool, split into two layers.

4 Chop the mint leaves in a food processor, then add the butter and sugar. Once the cake is cool, sprinkle the chocolate mint liqueur over both halves and sandwich together with the filling.

5 Put the butter, granulated sugar, liqueur and water into a small pan. Melt the butter and sugar, then boil for 5 minutes. Sieve the icing sugar and cocoa together and add the butter and liqueur mixture. Beat until cool and thick. Cover the cake with this mixture, and decorate with the pecan halves.

Strawberry Mint Sponge

This combination of fruit, mint and ice cream is a real winner.

1 CAKE

6-10 fresh mint leaves, plus more to decorate
170 g/6 oz/³⁄₄ cup caster sugar
170 g/6 oz/³⁄₄ cup butter, plus extra to grease tin
3 eggs
170 g/6 oz/1¹⁄₂ cups self-raising flour
1.2 litres/2 pints/2¹⁄₂ US pints strawberry ice cream
600 ml/1 pint/2¹⁄₂ cups double cream
2 tbsp mint liqueur
350 g/12 oz/2 cups fresh strawberries

1 Tear the mint into pieces and mix with the caster sugar. Leave overnight.

2 Grease and line a deep springform cake tin. Preheat the oven to 190°C/375°F/gas 5. Remove the mint from the sugar. Mix the butter and sugar and add the flour, then the eggs. Pile the mixture into the tin.

3 Bake for 20-25 minutes, or until a skewer or pointed knife inserted in the middle comes away clean. Turn out on to a wire rack to cool. When cool, carefully split horizontally into two equal halves.

4 Clean the cake tin and line it with clear non-PVC film. Put the bottom half of the cake back in the tin. Spread on the ice cream mixture and level the top. Put on the top half of the cake and freeze for 3-4 hours.

5 Whip the cream with the mint liqueur. Remove the cake from the freezer and quickly spread a layer of whipped cream all over it, leaving a rough finish. Put the cake back into the freezer until about 10 minutes before serving. Decorate the cake with the strawberries and place fresh mint leaves on the plate around the cake.

Carrot Cake with Geranium Cheese

At a pinch you can justify carrot cake as being good for you – at least this is an excuse for taking a good many calories on board. But the flavour is worth it.

1 CAKE

2-3 scented geranium leaves (preferably with a lemon scent)

225 g/8 oz/2 cups icing sugar

115 g/4 oz/1 cup self-raising flour

1 tsp bicarbonate of soda

½ tsp ground cinnamon

½ tsp ground cloves

200 g/7 oz/1 cup soft brown sugar

225 g/8 oz/1½ cups grated carrot

150 g/5 oz/½ cup sultanas

150 g/5 oz/½ cup finely chopped preserved stem ginger

150 g/5 oz/½ cup pecan nuts

150 ml/¼ pint/⅔ cup sunflower oil

2 eggs, lightly beaten

butter to grease tin

CREAM CHEESE TOPPING

60 g/2¼ oz/generous ¼ cup cream cheese

30 g/1¼ oz/2 tbsp softened butter

1 tsp grated lemon rind

1 Put the geranium leaves, torn into small- to medium-sized pieces, in a small bowl and mix with the icing sugar. Leave in a warm place overnight for the sugar to take up the scent of the leaves.

From left: *Lavender Cookies; Carrot Cake with Geranium Cheese*

2 Sift the flour, soda and spices together. Add the soft brown sugar, carrots, sultanas, ginger and pecans. Stir well then add the oil and beaten eggs. Mix with an electric beater for about 5 minutes, or 10-15 minutes longer by hand.

3 Preheat the oven to 180°C/350°F/ gas 4. Grease a 13 x 23 cm/5 x 9 in loaf tin, line the base with greaseproof paper, and then grease the paper. Pour the mixture into the pan and bake for about 1 hour. Remove the cake from the oven, leave to stand for a few minutes, and then turn it out on to a wire rack to cool.

4 While the cake is cooling, make the cream cheese topping. Remove the pieces of geranium leaf from the icing sugar and discard them. Place the cream cheese, butter and lemon rind in a bowl. Using an electric beater or a wire whisk, gradually add the icing sugar, beating well until smooth.

5 Once the cake has cooled, cover the top with the cream cheese mixture.

Lavender Cookies

Instead of lavender you can use any other flavouring, such as cinnamon, lemon, orange or mint.

ABOUT 30 BISCUITS

150 g/5 oz/⅝ cup butter, plus more to grease baking sheets

115 g/4 oz/½ cup granulated sugar

1 egg, beaten

1 tbsp dried lavender flowers

170 g/6 oz/1½ cups self-raising flour

leaves and flowers, to decorate

1 Preheat the oven to 180°C/350°F/ gas 4. Cream the butter and sugar together, then stir in the egg. Mix in the lavender flowers and the flour.

2 Grease two baking sheets and drop spoonfuls of the mixture on them. Bake for about 15-20 minutes, until the biscuits are golden. Serve with some fresh leaves and flowers to decorate.

Herbal Punch

A good party drink that will have people coming back for more, and a delightful non-alcoholic choice for drivers.

SERVES 30 PLUS

450 ml/³/₄ pint/2 cups honey

4 litres/7 pints/8½ US pints water

450 ml/³/₄ pint/2 cups freshly
   squeezed lemon juice

3 tbsp fresh rosemary leaves, plus
   more to decorate

1.5 kg/3½ lb/8 cups sliced
   strawberries

450 ml/³/₄ pint/2 cups freshly
   squeezed lime juice

1.75 litres/3 pints/4 US pints
   sparkling mineral water

ice cubes

3-4 scented geranium leaves

1 Combine the honey, 1 litre/1³/₄ pints/4½ cups water, one-eighth of the lemon juice, and the rosemary leaves in a saucepan. Bring to the boil, stirring until all the honey is dissolved. Remove from the heat and allow to stand for about 5 minutes. Strain into a large punch bowl.

2 Press the strawberries through a fine sieve into the punch bowl, add the rest of the water and lemon juice, and the lime juice and sparkling water. Stir gently. Add the ice cubes 5 minutes before serving, and float the geranium and rosemary leaves on the surface.

Angelica Liqueur

This should be drunk in tiny glasses after a large meal. Not only will it help the digestive system, it tastes superb.

ABOUT 1 LITRE

1 tsp fennel seeds

1 tsp aniseed

20 coriander seeds

2-3 cloves

2 tbsp crystallized angelica stems

225 g/8 oz/1 cup caster sugar

1 bottle vodka

1 Crush the fennel, aniseed and coriander seeds and cloves a little, and chop the crystallized angelica stems.

2 Put the seeds and angelica stems into a large preserving jar.

3 Add the sugar. Pour on the vodka and leave by a sunny window for 2 weeks, swirling the mixture daily.

4 Strain through fine muslin into a sterilized bottle and seal. Leave in a dark cupboard for at least 4 months. Drink in small quantities with a piece of angelica in each glass.

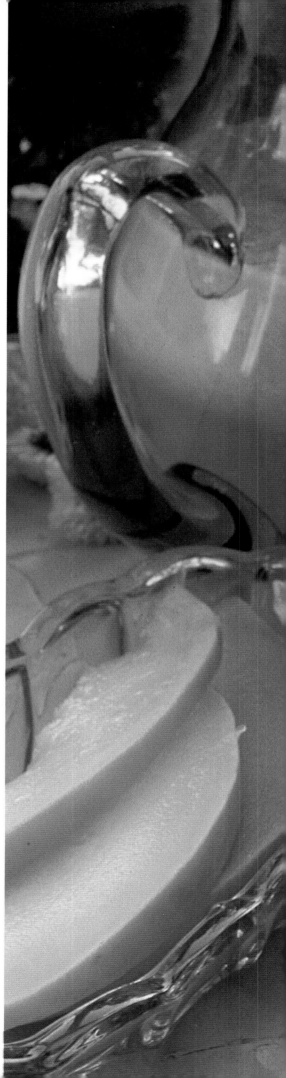

Strawberry and Mint Champagne

This is a simple concoction that makes a bottle of champagne go a lot further. It tastes very special on a hot summer's evening.

<small>SERVES 4-6</small>
500 g/1 lb strawberries
6-8 fresh mint leaves
1 bottle champagne or sparkling white wine

1 Purée the strawberries and mint leaves in a food processor.

2 Strain through a fine sieve into a bowl. Half fill a glass with the mixture and top up with champagne. Decorate with a sprig of mint.

Melon, Ginger and Borage Cup

Melon and ginger complement each other magnificently. If you prefer, you can leave out the powdered ginger – the result is milder but equally delicious.

<small>SERVES 6-8</small>
½ large honeydew melon
1 litre/1¾ pints/1 quart ginger beer
1 tsp powdered ginger (or to taste)
borage sprigs with flowers, to decorate

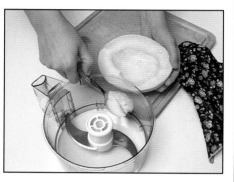

1 Discard the seeds from the half melon and scoop the flesh into a food processor. Blend to a thin purée.

2 Pour the purée into a large jug and top up with ginger beer. Add powdered ginger to taste. Pour into glasses and decorate with borage.

From left: *Melon, Ginger and Borage Cup; Strawberry and Mint Champagne*

Mint Cup

Mint is a perennially popular flavour and this delicate cup is a wonderful mixture with an intriguing taste.

SERVES 1

4 sprigs fresh mint

¹⁄₂ tsp sugar

crushed ice

¹⁄₂ tsp lemon juice

2 tbsp grapefruit juice

120 ml/4 fl oz/¹⁄₂ cup chilled tonic water

lemon slices, to decorate

1 Crush two of the sprigs of mint with the sugar and put these into a glass. Fill the glass with crushed ice.

2 Add the lemon juice, grapefruit juice and tonic water. Stir gently and decorate with the remaining mint sprigs and slices of lemon.

Elderflower Sparkler

The flavour of elderflowers is becoming popular once again. This recipe produces one of the most delicious drinks ever concocted. Many prefer it to real French champagne because of its light and refreshing taste.

ABOUT 5 LITRES/8½ PINTS/ 10 US PINTS

750 g/1¾ lb/3½ cups caster sugar

475 ml/16 fl oz/2 cups hot water

4 large fresh elderflower heads

2 tbsp white wine vinegar

juice and pared rind of 1 lemon

4 litres/7 pints/8½ US pints water

1 Mix the sugar with the hot water. Pour the mixture into a large glass or plastic container. Add all the remaining ingredients. Stir well, cover and leave for about 5 days.

2 Strain off the liquid into sterilized screw-top bottles (glass or plastic). Leave for a further week or so. Serve very cold with slivers of lemon rind.

Chamomile Tea

The pretty yellow flowers that are used for brewing this tea give the infusion a delicate colour.

SERVES 4

600 ml/1 pint/2½ cups boiling water
1 tbsp dried chamomile flower heads
caster sugar or honey (optional)

1 Put the chamomile flowers into a teapot or directly into a cup or mug. Pour on the boiling water and leave to infuse for about 5 minutes, or longer if you prefer a stronger flavour.

2 Strain the tea and, if you wish, add a small amount of caster sugar or honey and stir to dissolve.

OTHER HERBAL TEAS

- Iced mint tea with fresh lemon verbena.
- Mint and lavender flower tea, serve iced in summer.
- Marigold and lemon balm.

Blackcurrant and Lemon Verbena Tisane

 A warm, comforting fruity drink that will revive you on a cold winter's night. It is also excellent served chilled on a hot summer's day.

SERVES 4

600 ml/1 pint/2½ cups boiling water
1 tbsp fresh or frozen blackcurrants
10 lemon verbena leaves
brown sugar (optional)

1 Pour the boiling water over the blackcurrants and lemon verbena leaves and leave to infuse for about 5 minutes, or longer to taste.

2 Strain the liquid into cups or tall glasses and decorate with a sprig of lemon verbena. If you prefer a sweeter drink, stir in 1 tsp of brown sugar.

HERBS IN THE HOME

Fresh Herbal Wreath

This ring looks very attractive hanging in the kitchen. If you choose culinary herbs to include in the design, it can act as a dried herb store as well, and you can snip pieces off the ring to include in recipes as they are needed. The example is purely decorative, as the herbs are not usually needed for cooking.

hot glue gun

silver rose wire

'twiggy' wreath ring, approximately
  25 cm/10 in diameter

small bunches of whichever herbs are
  handy – this example includes leaves
  and sprigs of golden sage,
  chamomile, lavender, santolina,
  scented geranium

scissors

2 m/2 yd co-ordinating ribbon,
  2 cm/³⁄₄ in wide

1 Use the hot glue gun or wire to attach a good covering of golden sage and anthemis leaves to the wreath ring.

2 Make small bunches of the lavender and santolina, binding them with wire on to the wreath ring.

3 Choose the point where you want to attach the ribbons, and put three medium-sized scented geranium leaves here to act as a backing for the ribbon. Make double loops and streamers with the ribbon of your choice, bind them with wire and glue or wire them on to the ring. Other small flowers or herbs could also be fixed on as an extra. Once the herbs start to dry, keep adding more so that the ring becomes fuller and fuller. It will then eventually dry to a beautiful decoration.

Lavender Nosegay Pot

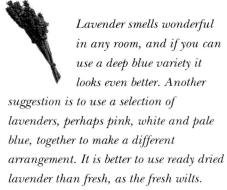

Lavender smells wonderful in any room, and if you can use a deep blue variety it looks even better. Another suggestion is to use a selection of lavenders, perhaps pink, white and pale blue, together to make a different arrangement. It is better to use ready dried lavender than fresh, as the fresh wilts.

terracotta pot
1 block grey florist's foam for dried
  flowers
4-5 large bunches lavender
scissors
1 m/1 yd ribbon
thin florist's wire (optional)

1 Press the foam into the pot. Decide on the height you would like the lavender and trim the stalks to that length, plus about 4 cm/2 in to go into the foam. Insert a small bunch into the centre of the pot.

2 Continue filling the pot tightly with lavender. It takes quite a few bunches to fill even a small pot, so have plenty to hand.

3 Once the pot is completely full and you cannot get another stem into the arrangement, wrap the ribbon around the top of the pot and tie a large bow. The ribbon used here was wired with thin florist's wire, which makes it easier to produce an attractive bow.

Tussie-Mussie

This delightful herbal posy is easily made and would make a delightful alternative to a bottle of wine as a gift to take to a dinner party.

6 Minuet roses
1 bunch southernwood
florist's wire
hellebore leaves
few stems of asparagus fern
posy frill
florist's tape
scissors
ribbon, as preferred

1 Take one of the roses and wrap some southernwood around it. Bind well with wire. Make up and add small bunches of hellebore leaves.

2 Add small wired bunches of southernwood and asparagus fern.

3 Continue to bind in more roses and greenery, until you are happy with the size and composition of the posy. Push the flowers through the center of the posy frill, secure with florist's tape and tie ribbons around it to decorate.

Rose and Herb Basket

Fresh flowers and herbs make a perfect partnership. The scent of the roses and herbs together is subtle but wonderful, especially if you hang the arrangement so that you brush lightly against it as you pass – but do not place it so that the roses are likely to be crushed. If you do not have the herbs listed here, there are many alternatives, for example sage and rosemary, and the leaves of any evergreen shrub.

1 block green florist's foam
small flower basket with handle
plastic sheet
florist's tape
scissors
hellebore leaves
scented geranium leaves
12 small sprays golden oregano
12 cream roses

1 Soak the florist's foam well. Line the basket with the plastic sheet so that no water will seep through the basketwork. Put the foam brick inside the liner and hold it in with tape. Cover the foam completely with a mixture of hellebore leaves and scented geranium leaves.

2 Add the sprays of golden oregano, placing them so that there will be room between them for the roses. Place the roses evenly throughout the arrangement, putting six on each side of the handle so that the arrangement looks well balanced, but not too symmetrical. Top up the foam with water each day to prolong the life of the arrangement.

Front to back: *Tussie-Mussie; Rose and Herb Basket*

Herbal Tablepiece

Extremely strong-smelling herbs should be avoided for table centres, as their fragrance may overpower the flavour of the meal. However, gently scented herbs make a delightful table decoration.

shallow basket without handle

2 blocks grey florist's foam for dried flowers

florist's wire

florist's tape

scissors

2 bunches cardoon thistles

3 large ivory candles

bunches of dried herbs, where possible in flower, including oregano, lavender, marjoram, fennel

1 Fill the basket with foam, wedging it into position. Group the cardoon heads into three positions in the foam. Make hairpins from wires, and tape three hairpins around the base of each candle. Place the candles into the foam.

2 Wire small bunches of lavender and marjoram, and spread evenly around the arrangement.

3 Place the fennel flower heads in the arrangement singly or wired together in groups, depending upon the space you wish to fill.

Caution: make sure that this arrangement is never left unattended with the candles alight.

Dried Herbal Topiary Tree

Topiary trees are an attractive way of displaying flowers and natural objects. This design includes small terracotta pots, which add to the textural interest in the top of the tree.

1 large terracotta pot for the base
cement or plaster of paris
piece of tree branch for the trunk
13 cm/5 in ball of grey florist's foam for dried flowers
small pieces of similar foam
2 large bunches of glycerined copper beech foliage or other preserved foliage
scissors
heavy-gauge florist's wire
wire cutters
12 miniature terracotta pots
2 bunches golden rod
light florist's wire
hot glue gun, if necessary
2 bunches poppy heads

1 Cover the hole in the large terracotta pot and half fill with wet cement or plaster of paris. As the cement begins to harden, stand the branch in the pot to form the trunk. Leave to dry for at least 48 hours before proceeding to next step.

2 Press the foam ball on to the trunk, making sure it is firmly in place, but not so far down that the trunk comes out the other side of the ball. Cover the cement in the base with pieces of foam.

3 Cover the ball and the base with pieces of copper beech or other preserved foliage. Thread heavy-gauge wire through the holes in the small pots and twist to make a stem so that they can be attached to the tree and pressed into the foam at the base.

4 Arrange the pots throughout the tree and base, and fill with small wired bunches of golden rod, trimming with scissors where needed. These can be glued into position if necessary, using the hot glue gun. Finally, add the poppy heads.

Herbal Christmas Wreath

Orange slices can be dried on a wire rack in an oven at the lowest possible setting for several hours until crisp.

They should then be carefully varnished to prevent reabsorption of moisture.

a few stems fresh holly

2 sprays fresh conifer

scissors

hot glue gun

wreath ring, approximately 9 in diameter

gold spray paint

2 in terracotta pot

broken pieces of terracotta pot

7 ears of wheat, sprayed gold

1 small bunch dried sage

1 small bunch oregano

florist's wire

3 dried orange slices

1 Attach the holly and conifer to the ring using the hot glue gun. Cover approximately half the ring.

2 In a well-ventilated area, spray a little gold paint on to the pot and pieces of pot and glue them to the design. Add the ears of wheat. Make small bunches of sage and tuck those among the pieces of broken pot.

3 Make a chunky bunch of the dried oregano, wiring it together. Glue into the main pot in the center of the design. Cut the orange slices into quarters and glue those into the arrangement. The fresh ingredients will dry on the wreath and look most attractive.

Dried Herbal Posy

This pretty posy could be given as a present or to say 'thank you'. It would also make a very pretty dressing table decoration. The ingredients are dried, so it can be made well in advance, or make a few to have to hand as gifts.

1 small bunch dried red roses

florist's wire

1 small bunch alchemilla

1 small bunch marjoram

cotton posy frill, deep pink

3 sprays dried bay

hot glue gun

florist's tape

scissors

ribbon, as preferred

1 Start with a small cluster of red roses, binding them with wire to form a center. Add some alchemilla, binding gently but firmly in the same spot.

2 Bind in some marjoram and then more red roses and alchemilla, until you are happy with the size of the posy. Push the stems of the posy through the center of the posy frill.

3 Separate the bay leaves from the stems and glue them in one at a time, through the arrangement and around the edge as a border.

4 Push the posy frill up towards the flowers and fasten with tape. Tie a length of ribbon around the stem of the posy and make a bow.

Scented and Decorated Candles

Candlelight is always a beautiful way of illuminating a room or dining table. Perfume can easily be added to candles by dropping a single drop of essential oil to the puddle of melted candle wax near the wick. These candles have been decorated with pressed herbs; the matching essential oil can be added later.

tall preserving jar, or other tall
 container
boiling water
large candles
pressed herbs, including geranium,
 lemon verbena, ivy, fennel flowers
essential oils of the herbs, as
 preferred

1 Fill the jar with boiling water. Decorating the candles one by one, dip a candle into the water, holding it by the wick, and keep it submerged for about one and a half minutes. Using tweezers, quickly press the leaves on to the softened wax.

2 Once the design is finished or the wax is no longer soft enough for the leaves to stick, immerse the candle in the boiling water again. This leaves a layer of wax over the design – the more you dip the candle, the further inwards the pressed leaves will move.

3 Make a set of several designs and display them in a group. Add one or more essential oils to the candles.

Herbal Pot-Pourri

Pot-pourri made at home bears no resemblance to the commercially manufactured variety. Using dried herbs you can quickly produce a mixture that smells wonderful and which will scent the room delightfully. Give it an occasional stir to release more fragrance.

1 handful dried mint leaves
2 handfuls dried marigold flowers
1 handful any other dried herbs, such
 as thyme, sage, marjoram
10 slices dried orange
6 cinnamon sticks
a few dried chillies
4 nutmegs
1 tsp mint essential oil
1 tbsp sweet orange
 essential oil
1 tbsp orris root
large metal or glass bowl
plastic bag

1 Mix all the ingredients, except for the orris root, together in the bowl – do not use a wooden or plastic one, as this will absorb the essential oils and will smell for a long time. Make sure the oils are well mixed with all the other ingredients.

2 Tip the mixture into a large plastic bag, add the orris root and shake well. Leave to mature for a week or two, shaking occasionally. Then tip the mixture into a suitable display bowl or dish. Remember that essential oils can damage a polished surface, so keep away from wooden table tops.

Front to back: *Herbal Pot-Pourri; Scented and Decorated Candles*

 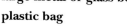

Herbal Moth Bags

Moths dislike any pungent herbal fragrance. Herbs such as tansy and southernwood work very effectively, but lavender is perhaps the most irritating to them, and the most pleasing to us.

2 cups dried lavender flowers
1 cup dried tansy leaves
2 cups dried southernwood
2 crushed cinnamon sticks
1 tsp orris root
small burlap bags
small rubber bands
ribbon or cord, as preferred

1 Mix all the ingredients together and bag them up in small hessian bags. Secure the necks with small rubber bands.

2 Decorate with cord or ribbons, and hang in wardrobes or place in drawers.

Herb Pillows and Cushions

Hop pillows have long been known for their sleep-inducing properties, but herbal mixtures are just as effective and can also be used to give a general fragrance to a room. This mixture is a useful basic recipe, but any dried herbs of your choice can be used.

1 cup dried mint
1 cup dried lavender
1 cup dried lemon verbena
1 cup dried lemon thyme
3 cups dried lemon scented geranium leaves
calico or muslin bags
rubber bands, or needle and thread
1 tsp orris root (optional)
1 tsp herbal essential oil (optional)
plastic bag

1 Mix all the ingredients together. Put them in the bags, and secure tightly with rubber bands or draw strings, or by sewing up the ends. Slip these herbal bags into pillows or cushions to give a gentle fragrance.

2 For a stronger smell, add 1 tsp of orris root and the same amount of any herbal essential oil. Leave the mixture to mature in a plastic bag for a week or two before using.

Lavender Sachets

Lavender sachets are always a welcome gift, and several sachets kept among the linen in the airing cupboard will impart a fragrance that makes clean sheets even more inviting.

small calico or muslin bags

lavender flowers

rubber bands

ribbon, as preferred

selection of dried flowers

hot glue gun

sprigs of dried herbs (optional)

1 Fill the bags with the dried lavender flowers, and secure with a rubber band. Do not overfill the bags, or they will be difficult to secure.

2 Tie the neck of the bag with a ribbon and decorate with a selection of dried flowers, attached with a hot glue gun. One of the most effective ways to decorate the bags is to use a couple of dried roses and perhaps a sprig of lavender or other herb.

Rosebud and Cardamom Pomander

These rosebud pomanders are fun to make and add a pretty touch to any room. They can be hung on a wall, or over a dressing-table mirror. When the colour has faded they can be sprayed gold as a Christmas ornament.

ribbon or cord for hanging

medium florist's wire

7.5 cm/3 in ball grey florist's foam for dried flowers

scissors

small rosebuds

general-purpose adhesive

green cardamom pods

1 Make a long loop with the ribbon or cord. Bind the base of the loop with wire. Leave a long end of wire, and push this through the centre of the ball and out through the other side. Trim the wire to about 2.5 cm/1 in long, and bend the end over to lose the end in the foam ball.

2 Stick the rosebuds into the foam by their stems. If they have no stems, use a little glue. Cover the entire ball with roses, pressing them close together to make sure that none of the foam is visible. Once the ball is completely covered, glue some green cardamom pods between the rosebuds to give a contrast in colour and texture.

Scented Wooden Brushes

Wooden brushes and accessories can be given a delightful fragrance with a very tiny amount of essential oil. Varnish is damaged by essential oils, so do not get any oil on the shiny back of the brush.

wooden hairbrush, unvarnished
essential oil, such as lavender
wooden hair clip, unvarnished

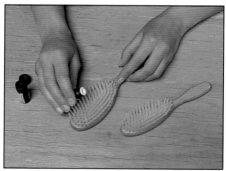

1 Take the wooden hairbrush and sprinkle two or three drops of your favourite essential oil on to the bristle side. The oil will be absorbed by the bristles and the wood, and will impart a fragrance for quite some time. When the scent fades, add a little more oil. As you brush your hair it will leave a lingering fragrance. Do not use too much oil, as this is messy and may also damage a polished surface.

2 To add more fragrance to your hair, sprinkle a couple of drops of essential oil on the wooden hair clip. This should be an unvarnished one, which will absorb the oil and will not be damaged by it.

Herb Corsages

Making your own buttonhole or corsage is easy. Tiny posy frills are obtainable from specialist floral suppliers, or you could use the centre of a paper doyley.

1 medium-sized flower

1 sprig any herb with attractive leaves

thin florist's wire

miniature posy frill, or cut-down doyley

florist's tape

1 For a centrepiece, you could use a rose or small spray carnation. Wrap some herb foliage around it – parsley would look good – and bind tightly with thin wire.

2 Push the stems through the centre of the frill and tape them together, covering the stems all the way down. Other combinations could include rosemary, sage, lavender or box.

Scented Valentine Heart

Valentine gifts in the shape of a heart are always popular. This heart-shaped gift box with dried flower and herb decoration on the lid is accompanied by a matching wreath made with fresh leaves and flowers that remain attractive when they dry.

heart-shaped box
broad and narrow ribbon
hot glue gun
5 dried roses
dried bay leaves
1 bunch dried golden rod
heart-shaped wreath form
houttuynia leaves
Minuet roses
1 sprig fresh lavender

1 Start decorating the gift box by making a large bow with broad ribbon. Then stick the dried ingredients on to the box to resemble a bunch of flowers. Stick the bow on top.

2 Wrap some narrow ribbon around the wreath form and secure with glue. Add a few houttuynia leaves (this variety is *H. cordata*), some Minuet roses and fresh lavender. These could be attached with wire instead of glue if you prefer.

Herb-Decorated Crackers

Home-made touches are important at Christmas, as they add the final touch to a family celebration. These crackers are easy to decorate and could be made by adults and children together. Buy ready-decorated crackers and remove the commercial trimming.

crackers

narrow ribbon, as preferred

scissors

small sprigs of various herbs, as preferred

hot glue gun, or general-purpose adhesive

1 Tie the ends of the crackers with ribbon, making attractive bows.

2 Make small posies of herbs and glue them to the middle part of the crackers.

Scented Pressed Herb Diary

A notebook or diary can be scented by placing it in a box with a strong lavender sachet, or a cotton-wool ball sprinkled with a few drops of essential oil. Leave it in the sealed box for a month or so to impart a sweet lingering fragrance. Another idea is to wipe the inside of the covers lightly with a small amount of essential oil on a lint pad. Try to find a very plain diary or notebook which does not have lettering or decoration on the cover, as these would spoil the design. Use a plastic film made for covering books. Some types are ironed on, others cling by themselves.

**pressed leaves and flowers, such as
  borage flowers, alchemilla flowers
  and small leaves, daisies, single
  roses, forget-me-nots**
plain diary or notebook
tweezers
large tapestry needle
white latex adhesive
clear plastic film
iron and cloth pad, if required

1 Start by arranging a selection of pressed leaves on the front of the diary or notebook, using the tweezers for positioning.

2 Continue to build up your design by adding the pressed flower heads.

3 Once you are happy with the design stick it down, using a large tapestry needle and latex adhesive. Slide the needle into the glue and then, without moving the design, place a small amount of glue under each leaf and petal so that they are secure. Cover with clear film. If the film needs heating, iron gently with a cloth pad between the film and the iron.

Pressed Herb Cards

A home-made card is always one that will be treasured long after the occasion has passed. Although it takes time and trouble to make your own cards, you could make a batch and keep them for a suitable occasion. It is always worth the effort to give someone something with your personal touch.

**pressed herbs and flowers, such as
  blue cornflower, ivy, rosemary,
  borage**
blank greeting card
large tapestry needle
white latex adhesive
clear plastic film
iron and cloth pad, if required

1 Arrange a selection of pressed herbs and flowers on the front of the card, using tweezers for positioning.

2 When the design is complete, stick it down, using a large tapestry needle and latex adhesive. Using the needle, slide small dabs of adhesive beneath the herbs and flowers without altering their position. Cover with a clear film. If the film needs heating, iron gently with a cloth pad between the film and the iron.

Right: *assorted Pressed Herb Cards and Scented Pressed Herb Diaries*

Chamomile and Honey Mask

Although this mask makes you look a little strange while it is on your face, it smooths and softens skin beautifully. Chamomile flowers are usually easy to obtain from a health food shop as they are often used for making chamomile tea.

1 tbsp dried chamomile flowers
175 ml/6 fl oz/³/₄ cup boiling water
2 tbsp bran
1 tsp clear honey, warmed

1 Pour the boiling water over the chamomile flowers and allow them to stand for 30 minutes. Then strain the infusion and discard the chamomile flowers.

2 Mix 3 tbsp of the liquid with the bran and honey and rub this mixture all over your face. It may be a little stiff at first but will smooth out over the skin. Leave the mixture on your skin for at least 10 minutes, then rinse off with warm water.

Tansy Skin Tonic

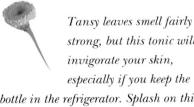

Tansy leaves smell fairly strong, but this tonic will invigorate your skin, especially if you keep the bottle in the refrigerator. Splash on this cool herbal liquid to start the day.

1 large handful tansy leaves
150 ml/¹⁄₄ pint/²⁄₃ cup water
150 ml/¹⁄₄ pint/²⁄₃ cup milk

1 Put the leaves, water and milk in a small pan and bring to the boil. Simmer for 15 minutes, then allow to cool in the pan.

2 Strain the tonic into a bottle. Keep the mixture in the refrigerator, and apply cold to the skin as a soothing toner or tonic.

Feverfew Complexion Milk

Feverfew grows prolifically in the garden, self-seeding all over the herb beds, and this is a welcome use for some of this over-enthusiastic plant. The milk will moisturize dry skin, help to fade blemishes, and discourage blackheads.

1 large handful feverfew leaves
300 ml/½ pint/1¼ cups milk

1 Put the leaves and milk in a small saucepan and simmer for 20 minutes.

2 Allow the mixture to cool in the pan then strain into a bottle. Keep it in the refrigerator.

FEVERFEW FLOWERS

• Feverfew can be cultivated easily; it is especially pretty grown in tubs and pots in the greenhouse or conservatory.

• Hang bunches of flowers upside down and leave to air-dry; use as a decorative addition to dried flower arrangements.

Fennel Cleanser

Fennel is another herb that self-seeds all over the garden, so once you have planted it supplies will be no problem. The leaves have an aniseed aroma. This mixture gently but thoroughly cleanses the day's grime away.

1 tbsp fennel seed
250 ml/8 fl oz/1 cup boiling water
1 tsp honey
2 tbsp buttermilk

1 Lightly crush the fennel seeds, pour on the boiling water and allow to infuse for about 30 minutes.

2 Strain the cooled liquid into a small bowl and add the honey and buttermilk. Transfer to a clean bottle and keep the mixture refrigerated.

FENNEL SEEDS

- The tall, graceful heads of fennel seeds add height to a cottage herb garden. The seeds are valued for their distinctive aroma. In Victorian times the seeds came to symbolize the virtue of strength.
- At one time, fennel seeds were combined with those of dill and caraway in little sacks or purses, to be chewed at prayer meetings to quell hunger pangs: they were known as 'meeting seeds'.

Parsley Hair Tonic

Parsley stimulates the scalp and gets the circulation going, which aids hair growth and adds shine.

1 large handful parsley sprigs
2 tbsp water

1 Place the parsley sprigs and water in a food processor.

2 Process until ground to a smooth purée. Apply the green lotion to the scalp, then wrap your head in a warm towel and leave for about 1 hour before shampooing as normal.

Lemon Verbena Hair Rinse

Add a delicious fragrance to your hair with this rinse. It will also stimulate the pores and circulation. Lemon verbena is worth growing in the garden, if only so that you can walk past and pick a wonderfully scented leaf.

1 handful lemon verbena leaves
250 ml/8 fl oz/1 cup boiling water

1 Pour the boiling water over the lemon verbena leaves and leave to soak for at least 1 hour.

2 Strain the mixture and discard the leaves. Pour this rinse over your hair after conditioning.

From left: *Lemon Verbena Hair Rinse; Parsley Hair Tonic*

Chamomile Conditioning Rinse

Chamomile flowers help to keep blonde hair a bright, clear colour. They will not lift the colour in hair that is medium to dark, but will help to brighten naturally fair hair, as well as leaving a pleasant fragrance.

125 ml/4 fl oz/½ cup chamomile flowers
600 ml/1 pint/2½ cups water
1 handful scented geranium leaves

1 Place the flowers and water in a saucepan and bring to the boil. Simmer for approximately 15 minutes.

2 While the liquid is still hot, strain on to the scented geranium leaves. Leave to soak for 30-40 minutes. Strain again, this time into a bottle. Use the mixture after shampooing.

Rosemary Hair Tonic

Rosemary is an excellent substitute for mildly medicated shampoos, and this tonic also helps control greasy hair and enhances the shine and natural colour.

250 ml/8 fl oz/1 cup fresh rosemary
   tips
1.2 litres/2 pints/5 cups bottled
   water

1 Put the ingredients in a saucepan and bring to the boil. Simmer for approximately 20 minutes, then allow to cool in the pan.

2 Strain the mixture and store it in a clean bottle. Use after shampooing the hair.

Herbal Bath Bags

These are much more fun than putting commercial bubble bath into the water. Tie them over the taps and make sure the hot running water is going through them – this will release lovely herbal scents that relax and comfort you.

3 x 23 cm/9 in diameter circles of muslin

6 tbsp bran

1 tbsp lavender flowers

1 tbsp chamomile flowers

1 tbsp rosemary tips

3 small rubber bands

3 m/3 yd narrow ribbon or twine

1 Place 2 tbsp bran in the centre of each circle of muslin. Add the lavender to one bag, the chamomile to a second and the rosemary to the third.

2 Gather each circle of material up and close with a rubber band. Then tie a reasonable length of ribbon or twine around each bag to make a loop so that the bag can be hung from the hot tap in the stream of water.

Rose Hand Cream

This is an excellent scented hand cream which softens and moisturizes.

1 tsp beeswax

¼ tsp honey

4 tbsp almond oil

4 tbsp rosewater

1 Put the beeswax, honey and almond oil in a glass jar standing in a small pan of hot water. Stir until melted and blended.

2 Stir vigorously while pouring in the rosewater. Take the jar out of the water, and continue to stir gently until the mixture has cooled.

Dill Aftershave

Most recipes are for fragrances for women, so here is one for men. It is best kept in the refrigerator so that the cool liquid has a bracing effect as well as smelling good.

50 g/2 oz/¼ cup dill seed
1 tbsp honey
600 ml/1 pint/2½ cups bottled water
1 tbsp distilled witch hazel

1 Place the dill seed, honey and water in a small saucepan and bring to the boil. Simmer for about 20 minutes.

2 Allow to cool in the pan, then add the witch hazel. Strain the cooled mixture into a bottle and refrigerate.

Lavender Bubble Bath

There is no need to buy commercially made bubble baths again. This fragrance is quite delicious and so simple to make that you can make some spares as gifts for friends and family – you will be in great demand!

1 bunch lavender
clean wide-necked jar, with screw top
1 large bottle clear organic shampoo
5 drops oil of lavender

1 Place the bunch of lavender head downwards in the jar. If the stalks are longer than the jar cut them down, as it is the flowers that do the work. Add the shampoo and the lavender oil.

2 Close the jar and place on a sunny window sill for 2-3 weeks, shaking occasionally.

3 Strain the liquid and re-bottle. Use about 1 tbsp in a bath.

Dandelion Tea

Most warm herbal teas have a comforting effect. Dandelions are a diuretic, and can help to reduce water retention and bloated feelings. Many people find that this is a useful treatment for rheumatism. This tea also acts as a mild laxative so should not be drunk in large quantities.

5-6 dandelion leaves

boiling water

1 tsp honey (optional)

1 Remove any stems from the dandelion leaves. Break them into strips and place in the bottom of a mug. Pour on enough boiling water to fill the mug and leave to stand for 5-10 minutes.

2 Strain, discard most of the dandelion leaves, and drink. If you prefer a sweeter brew, add a small teaspoonful of honey.

DANDELIONS

- Dandelion roots when dried can be used as a coffee substitute; they can also be added to beer and wine.
- Dandelion leaves are eaten as a salad vegetable in Mediterranean countries; they can also be blanched and served as a cooked accompaniment.

Thyme Tea

Thyme is excellent for treating chest infections and coughs. This tea is a comforting extra treatment, but do not rely on it to cure. However, it will help to combat sleeplessness and irritating coughs.

25g/1 oz fresh thyme
600 ml/1 pint/2½ cups boiling water
honey

1 Take the fresh thyme and cover with the boiling water. Allow to infuse for at least 5-10 minutes, to taste.

2 Add a little honey, and drink while still piping hot.

DECORATIVE THYME

- Collect and air-dry bunches of thyme when in flower. The flowers can be used in dried floral arrangements.
- Alternatively, when the flowers are dry, crumble them between your fingertips and add to pot-pourri mixtures.

Lavender and Marjoram Bath

A long warm bath is an excellent way of relieving the stresses and strains of a busy day. This bath mixture has the added bonus of moisturizing the skin while it gently soothes away cares and troubles. The essential oils induce sleep. To enhance the effect, you could add a bath bag containing fresh lavender and marjoram to the water.

2 tbsp almond oil
7 drops lavender oil
3 drops marjoram oil

1 Measure out all the ingredients into a small dish or bowl.

2 Mix all the ingredients together and pour them into the bath while the water is running, then have a long, soothing soak.

Lemon Grass, Coriander and Clove Bath

If you are suffering from stiff limbs after excessive exercise, this bath will help stimulate the circulation and relieve suffering in joints and muscles.

2 tbsp almond oil
2 drops lemon grass oil
2 drops coriander oil
2 drops clove oil

1 Carefully measure the almond oil into a small dish.

2 Slowly drop in all the essential oils. Mix all the ingredients and pour into the bath while the water is running. Rinse the dish under the running tap to make sure all the oils have gone into the bath water. Take a long, relaxing bath.

Lavender Oil

Lavender oil is the most useful of all the essential oils, and perhaps the safest. Allergic reaction is virtually unknown and, unlike many of the other essential oils, it is safe to apply it directly to the skin.

It can help to promote sleep – sprinkle a few drops on to the pillow, or on to a handkerchief placed on the pillow, for adults and children to enjoy untroubled rest.

It is also excellent for treating burns, stings, scalds and minor wounds. Deter flying insects by rubbing the essential oil into uncovered parts of the body, such as hands and feet, on a warm evening when sitting outside.

Lavender oil can be added to bottled water (about 6 drops to 600 ml/1 pint/2½ cups) and sprinkled on to dry pillow cases or any other linen before ironing to leave a lingering fragrance.

From left: *Lemon Grass, Coriander and Clove Bath; Lavender and Marjoram Bath*

Comfrey Infusion

This is a useful lotion to make up to treat minor cuts and scrapes. It should be used at room temperature when not too cold, as it is more soothing warm.

2 tsp fresh comfrey leaves (or 1 tsp dried comfrey)
300 ml/½ pint/1¼ cups boiling water

1 Shred the fresh comfrey leaves into small pieces and cover with the boiling water. Allow to steep for 10 minutes. Leave to cool.

2 Gently bathe cuts and abrasions with this lotion on a lint pad. It is also good for minor burns, scalds and sunburn.

Mint Footbath and Massage Oil

After a long day on your feet, try soaking them in this soothing footbath. Then rub the mint oil into your feet to smooth and soften before you go to bed. The mint essential oil also has a refreshing scent.

MINT BATH

12 large sprigs mint

120 ml/4 fl oz/½ cup cold water

2.4 litres/4 pints/10 cups boiling water

MASSAGE OIL

1 tbsp almond oil

1 drop mint essential oil

1 Place the mint in a food processor and add the cold water. Process well until it becomes a green purée. Pour this into a large bowl and add the boiling water. Once the mixture has cooled to a bearable temperature, soak both feet at once until the water is too cool to be comforting.

2 Gently rub your feet dry with a soft towel. Mix the almond oil and the mint essential oil and rub well into both feet.

Index